CHOICE AND CHANCE

CHOICE AND CHANCE

A Libertarian Analysis

by

K. W. RANKIN

Senior Lecturer in Philosophy
University of Malaya

OXFORD
BASIL BLACKWELL
1961

FIRST PUBLISHED 1961
© BY BASIL BLACKWELL AND MOTT LTD.

PRINTED IN GREAT BRITAIN IN THE CITY OF OXFORD
AT THE ALDEN PRESS
BOUND BY THE KEMP HALL BINDERY, OXFORD

TO
O.S.R. AND O.T.R.

ACKNOWLEDGMENTS

THE earliest draft of the present work took form during my tenure of a Junior Research Fellowship in Philosophy (1951-53) awarded by Edinburgh University Grants Committee. Mr Peter Heath and Mr Eric Toms have restrained me from perpetrating many errors but have no complicity in those that remain. The editors of *Mind*, *The Philosophical Quarterly*, and *The Indian Journal of Philosophy* have kindly allowed me to use material from certain articles of mine which they have published. Mrs Joyce Wikkramatileke has done most of the typing. To all of those as well as to others who have in various ways assisted me in writing this book I wish to express my gratitude, and finally to my wife, I owe the amenity of unperturbed study to her industry and talent.

CONTENTS

INTRODUCTION

THE Indo-European tradition in philosophy may be viewed as an unremittant if somewhat ineffectual struggle to assimilate the concept of substance or thinghood. Philosophers who think traditionally have been preoccupied mainly with the unity in the plurality of events which pertain to the same thing, or with some such question as 'What is the subject of change?' So far the bane of this ontological pursuit has been chronic conjunctivitis. Plurality is baffling and unity elusive because of our inherent bias towards detailing any kind of variety extensively in terms of the conjunction 'and'. How natural it is to say, for instance, 'The same piece of wax was hard and then became soft, etc.', and then to imagine that the problem of unity or identity can be stated solely in these terms! But some kinds of variety should, on the contrary, be detailed *disjunctively* in terms of the exclusive 'or'. We must think more thoroughly in terms of indeterminacy or mutually exclusive possibilities. We fail to assimilate this concept so long as we imagine that its more important applications are confined to card-shuffling, dice-throwing, the jigging of sub-atomic particles, etc.

Two opposing accounts of substance illustrate the bias towards conjunction very clearly. At the risk of seeming to superimpose a number of slightly different problems I shall call them 'realistic' and 'phenomenalistic' respectively. The realistic method is to take the thing as something *additional to* the plurality of incidents which pertain to it, and to mark its obvious disparity in a figurative manner by describing the thing as underlying the incidents, as substance, or substratum, or an 'I know not what' support of qualities. Reality, accordingly, is considered to be the incidents *and* what lies beneath them. The phenomenalistic method is, or rather was originally, to treat the thing as nothing but the conjunction of incidents constituting its life history, as, according to one version, a family of sense-data. A more considered form of the same method is to reduce all categorical statements about material objects to conjunctions of conditional statements about sense-data.

I

This universal addiction to conjunction can be illustrated equally well by almost parallel accounts of the powers, forces, and dispositions which are exercised by or pertain to things. Sometimes they are identified with some sort of event analogous to muscular strain, or feeling of effort, which is additional to the other events associated with the thing. At other times an analysis is given of categorical statements about them in terms of conjunctions of hypothetical statements about events. The same opposing tendencies are also to be found in the analysis of personality, which is a special form of thinghood. Sometimes personality is attributed to a soul or a self which is additional to its mental states while at the same time underlying them. Sometimes it is simply identified with the conjunction of all these states. Again the peculiarly human type of power known as 'will' or 'conation' is sometimes identified with an event additional to other mental events. At other times statements about it are analysed into conjunctions of hypothetical statements about the person.

Another indication of just how rudimentary this conjunctive tendency is can be found in grammar and modern logic. Grammarians have classified both 'and' and 'or' as conjunctions. Modern logic corrects the mistake by subsuming both under the head of logical constants and by confining the label 'conjunction' to the former constant alone. Ever since its early affair with logical atomism, however, logic has perpetuated the mistake at a more fundamental level by showing a predilection for the extensional interpretation of its constants. For instance, the constants 'or' and 'if ... then' have usually been interpreted in the truth-functional manner as reducible to conjunctions of propositions about the truth or falsity of certain more elementary propositions. Thus 'if p then q' is interpreted as simply meaning 'It is not the case that p is true *and* q is false'. No doubt this is the most convenient interpretation for certain purposes but it remains provocative of ontological error.

I am not about to give a historical résumé or even a systematic analysis of thinghood. My direct concern is with the indeterminacy which is basic to practical knowledge and patent in our immediate experience of action once certain conceptual misunderstandings have been removed. To eradicate misunderstanding completely we should, indeed, dismantle one conceptual framework and erect another in its place. If a slogan is needed to give us heart, let us hazard that conjunctive pluralism must be replaced by disjunctive pluralism. But this programme is an ambitious one, which on the most lenient estimate the following analysis of action has only fulfilled in part by suggesting the need and direction for a conceptual reorientation. I begin by exploring some difficulties in the indeterministic interpretation of action which I favour.

CHAPTER I

THE LIBERTARIAN PARADOX

W E commonly suppose that among successively occurring events some have been causally conditioned, or determined, or necessitated by yet others. Sometimes we think of the necessary connection between two successive events as unique and reciprocal. On this way of thinking the antecedent of the two must be followed by the subsequent event, and the latter must be preceded by the former. At other times we think in J. S. Mill's terms, of a plurality of causes and effects, as if one of two successive events is necessarily but not uniquely connected with the other, so that relative to one the occurrence of each of a number of incompatible events is equally possible. We speak in some such way as 'This could have come about in more ways than one' or 'It is uncertain what effects this will have'. The occurrence of any one of the equally possible but incompatible events is, accordingly, indeterminately conditioned by the event relative to which it is possible.

Now we may try to give precedence to one of these two ways of thinking by supposing that the one way represents the detail of everything that happens more accurately than the other. Alternatively we may hold that each way represents the detail only of some of the things that happen more accurately than the other, and that neither represents accurately the detail of everything that happens. Both these attempts at generalization lead to the contrast between two familiar cosmological theories which can be formulated quite briefly and with negligible lack of finesse as follows.

Determinism (Mechanism) — In the succession of events which constitute any isolable system each event is in unique and reciprocal necessary relation in every respect both to antecedent and subsequent events (if there are any) with a zero range of indeterminacy.

Indeterminism — In the succession of events which constitute any isolable system some events are not in a unique and reciprocal necessary relation of the kind specified above.

Determinism has lost some of the attraction it formerly held in the hey-day of classical or pre-quantum mechanics. It is not dissimilar, however, from certain specific forms of Indeterminism which in basing more moderate claims upon the same sort of warrant have inherited some of the attraction which Determinism has lost. The similarity consists in giving necessary causal connection of the unique and reciprocal kind some useful though possibly inaccurate application within the universe, and the issue is just where to stop short. In many ways, in so far as this question has not already been answered, it is a matter for further scientific research rather than philosophical analysis. In the area of voluntary action with which I am now primarily concerned the latter method is, however, more appropriate.

Our problem is 'What forms of necessary causal connection are applicable to voluntary action?' To solve it we can for convenience scale down the scope of the various cosmological theories and confine them to the limits, whatever these are, within which voluntary action falls. Suppose, for instance, the action of rescuing a drowning man rather than remaining inactive is in unique and reciprocal necessary relation to antecedent events in and around the agent, but that the precise number of hairs by which he happens to grip the drowning man's head is not. I shall describe this supposition as a deterministic one on the grounds that the element of indeterminacy which it allows is irrelevant to voluntary action as such. Suppose by contrast that the precise number of hairs which he seizes is in unique reciprocal necessary relation to antecedent events once the agent takes the course of rescuing rather than of remaining inactive, but that his taking the one course rather than the other is not so determined. I shall describe this supposition as indeterministic on the grounds that the unique reciprocal necessary relation it allows is irrelevant to voluntary action.

Within these more manageable limits let us now discriminate more finely. I shall assume provisionally that the temporal order of events and the necessary relation between them are logically independent: though this assumption comes in for drastic revision in Chapter IX. In the meantime it seems possible to distinguish between four ways in which events may be necessarily connected. First, there is the strict deterministic relation in which events are connected in a unique and reciprocal manner. The other three are all indeterministic and I shall try and illustrate them first by means of examples from the field of action. These illustrations are, however, entirely question-begging at this stage, particularly since we may find later that some of the relations which I seek to illustrate are conceptually impossible.

Suppose to begin with that when an agent is faced by a choice, when for example Caesar paused at the Rubicon, the complete causal conditions determine a number of specific but incompatible courses of action as open to him. Each of the courses in this group is in addition made possible by that same complete set of antecedent causal conditions and no other. As possibilities, in other words, they are uniquely conditioned. But none of these courses is made necessary as distinct from possible by any antecedent condition no matter how completely one specifies the antecedent conditions. Thus let us suppose that once he had marched to the northern bank of the river Caesar had either to cross or to stay put or to turn in one direction or another. Further, he could not have done any of these things unless he had previously marched to the northern bank of the river: and no particular course out of this group necessarily follows from the march to the northern bank, even if one includes every contemporaneous physical and psychological event. Here then we have an example of the uniquely conditioned sort of indeterminacy postulated by the form of Indeterminism which is often called 'Libertarianism'.

Suppose, secondly, that there may be a particular event in the history of each one of us which will occur no matter which of a number of previous courses of action we happen to take. We can describe this event as our destiny or fate. Thus we can suppose that Caesar would have been assassinated on the Ides of March in the year 44 B.C. in precisely the same circumstances whether he had crossed the Rubicon or stayed put for some time or turned aside in one direction or another. (I leave aside the question whether these courses were open to him in terms of antecedent conditions as the Libertarians suggest.) The form of Fatalism which I have in mind, however, is highly specific. The destined or fated event leaves open the possibility of a specific group of antecedent incompatible events, but the possibility of any one of these antecedent events is dependent upon the destined event and

no other — or at least upon no other event later than the antecedent events. Here then is an example of a uniquely conditioned
indeterminacy different from the Libertarian kind.

Finally, for the sake of completeness suppose that a man has
alternative destinies. Either of two incompatible events must
happen to him no matter which event out of a specific group of
incompatible antecedent events has previously occurred. We may
suppose that whatever course he took at the Rubicon, Caesar had
either to die on the Ides of March or become first Emperor of the
Roman Empire. In addition we may suppose that either of the
two later events alone allows the antecedent causal possibility of
each one of the incompatible courses of action at the Rubicon.
We have postulated in other words two reciprocally conditioning
indeterminacies.

There are then four co-ordinate modes of necessary connection,
one of which is deterministic and three indeterministic. In future
I shall refer to them as one-one, one-many, many-one, and many-
many. This is a fairly obvious refinement on Mill's distinction
between plurality of causes and effects. Note that as with Mill the
plurality or many is a disjunctive and not a conjunctive plurality.
Its individual members are, in other words, mutually incompatible with each other.

The one-one, one-many, many-one distinction was, of course,
first devised by Russell but given a narrower more specialized
application than I now wish to give it. The father of many children
for instance is as a father in a one-many relation to his children:
but we must note that here the children are a conjunctive plurality,
e.g. Tom, Dick, and Harry. Also I have for the moment distinguished one-many from many-one in a different way from
Russell. According to him a relation is one-many where the term
which has that relation (the referent) is single and the term to
which it has the relation (the relatum) is plural. Contrariwise it is
many-one when the referent is plural and the relatum singular. I
on the other hand have for the moment distinguished between
the two less satisfactorily according to whether the single term
is earlier or later in time than any constituent of the plural term.

In view of these discrepancies it might, indeed, seem less misleading if I were to devise a different terminology from Russell's.
But any alternative device could only turn out to be a less succinct

though a fairly obvious periphrasis of the same essential ideas and consequently a somewhat craven capitulation before the conjunctive bias by which the interpretation of these technical terms has hitherto been limited.

We can now formulate the problem for solution in later chapters with greater precision. The two main theories about necessary connection between events, viz. Determinism and Indeterminism, exhaust the theories which on our assumptions are logically possible. Each contradicts the other. Accordingly, since we have restricted their scope to voluntary actions, voluntary action must take place, in conformity with one or other of these two theories. If we don't give a deterministic account of voluntary action we must adopt Indeterminism. On the other hand can any theory of action, such as Libertarianism professes to be, afford to be a form of Indeterminism? To be a theory of action at all Libertarianism must give some account of human responsibility. After all we do hold people responsible for what they do voluntarily. Hence, it is frequently alleged that as a form of Indeterminism Libertarianism is in fact self-contradictory, since the particular form of Indeterminism with which it is usually identified specifically rules out the responsibility of the agent for his action.

To examine more carefully the justice of this claim let us first reconsider the precise type of Indeterminism which Libertarianism must entail. I have already identified Libertarianism with the postulate of a one-many necessarily relationship in our actions, but actually a less rigid form of indeterminacy seems to be just as consistent with the openness of choice which the Libertarian wishes to explain. Provisionally we may say that he must believe that

(*a*) the indeterminacy postulated is of a limited kind;
(*b*) that it is either one-many or many-many in structure, but certainly not many-one.

Condition (*a*) recognizes that, without a limit to the range of indeterminacy in the future at the moment of action, choice — or at least human choice — would be impossible. This limitation need not, of course, be a limitation in the number of alternatives open for choice. Since space is infinitely divisible Caesar, for instance, could have behaved voluntarily in an infinite number of ways on pausing at the Rubicon — provided of course he had been equipped with the requisite niceties of perception and muscular control. Yet even under such ideal conditions the infinity of ways in which he could have acted was limited. He was incapable of taking the shortest cut to divinity by ascending vertically into the heavens: otherwise, no doubt, he would have done so. Similarly he was incapable of descending into the bowels of the earth — at least without a considerable amount of labour.

Accordingly, although the number of alternatives open in any situation may be infinite, they still exclude as causally impossible a further infinite number of imaginable alternatives. Without this limitation to the possibilities of action there would be no necessity whatever to take the situation and its causal properties into consideration at the moment of action in order to form and execute one's purpose. Action would become as simple as day-dreaming where the limitations of actual situations are ignored.

Condition (*b*) recognizes that the future alone is subject to the agent's choice, and not the past. While expiring on the Ides of March in the year 44 B.C. Caesar did not have a choice as to which of a number of incompatible trains of events should lead up to his destiny as his past. This I take to be a tautology rather than a contingent fact: but as in the instance of condition (*a*), I am concerned with its truth just now rather than with its logical status. If, then, we assume with the Libertarian that whatever is chosen must fall within a range of indeterminacy, this indeterminacy must characterize what at the moment of choice is the future. The fact that the future alone is subject to choice cannot, of course, be cited as sufficient evidence for the indeterminacy of the future without at this stage begging the question.

These two basic tenets of Libertarianism, then, definitely make it a form of Indeterminism: and it can be seen that by adhering to this particular form the Libertarian has not escaped the charge of inconsistency mentioned above. This charge presupposes that the relation of necessary connection between events is identical with the relationship of responsibility for something, or efficacy, which is inherent in voluntary action. Accordingly, if one supposes that one determinate group of events is necessarily connected, in accordance with conditions (*a*) and (*b*), with any one but no more than one group out of a limited range of subsequent groups, an

B

awkward conclusion must follow. The antecedent group of events must be responsible for the fact that nothing *outside* the limited range of subsequent groups occurs. On the other hand, it cannot be responsible for one event or group of events within the limited range occurring rather than another from the same range. Thus, if we identify responsibility with necessary connection, Caesar must, according to the Libertarian, be responsible for the fact that he had either to cross the Rubicon, remain where he was, or turn aside, but not for his having in fact taken the most ambitious course instead of being deterred by his scruples. But this implication is paradoxical, since we hold Caesar responsible for doing one of the actions *rather than* any of the others. Some, then, infer that Libertarianism cannot give an adequate account of responsibility or of being an agent.

There are a number of equivalent ways in which essentially the same criticism of Libertarianism can be and has been made. It will be instructive to consider some of these, since they bring out the close relation between the use of the terms 'responsibility', 'chance', 'accident', and 'randomness', as well as the ambiguities peculiar to each.

Bradley, for instance, writes:[1]

> The theory was to save responsibility. It saves it thus. A man is responsible because there was no reason why he should have done one thing, rather than another thing. And that man and only that man is responsible concerning whom it is impossible for anyone, even himself, to know what in the world he will be doing next, possible only to know what his actions are, when once they are done, and to know that they might have been the diametrical opposite. So far is such an account from saying responsibility (as we commonly understand it) that it annihilates the very conditions of it. It is the description of a person who is not responsible, who (if he is anything) is idiotic.

This quotation has the peculiar value of showing how the issue we have been considering can easily become confused with certain others.

The fourth sentence onwards seems based on an assumption that knowledge of the future consists in all cases of inference from

[1] *Ethical Studies*: The Vulgar Notion of Responsibility, p. 12.

data given at the moment and that this data is consistent with only one conclusion. My analysis of intending and predicting in Chapter VI onwards will show that this is open to question. The third sentence, however, is of more immediate relevance here. Bradley apparently confuses 'reason' meaning 'cause' with 'reason' meaning 'ground' or 'motive': for it is in the first sense of 'reason' that Libertarians must deny that voluntary actions have reasons.[1] They would never wish to claim that such actions must be unmotivated, without purpose, or aimless.

Bradley puts his point rather more effectively in another passage[2] where he explicitly attacks the Libertarianism of William James.

> But 'chance' appears with Professor James to have several senses. In his *Will to Believe* (p. 155) it is said to mean that under absolutely identical conditions the same result need not follow. This is, as I understand it, really to contend that the same A is at once and in precisely the same sense both B and not B, a contention which obviously would destroy and remove the whole notion of truth.

In this passage the central concept has changed from responsibility to its contradictory chance. If responsibility is identical with necessary connection then chance is identical with the absence of that necessary connection. Bradley has here insisted on the strict implications of the words 'conditions' and 'results'. If under absolutely identical circumstances either of two events may follow, then neither of the two events can have in these circumstances a sufficient condition: to that extent neither can be a result of anything.

More recently Ayer has written:[3]

> ... if it is not an accident that I choose to do one thing rather than another, then presumably there is some causal explanation of my choice.

And even more recently J. L. Mackie asks[4]

---

[1] Cf. Maurice Cranston, *Freedom*, pp. 169ff, with whose comments on this and other passages I am in substantial agreement.
[2] *Collected Essays*, vol. 2, p. 452 *passim*.
[3] *Polemic* 5, p. 39. Cf. also *Foundations of Empirical Knowledge*, chap. IV, p. 209.
[4] 'Evil and Omnipotence', *Mind*, April 1955, p. 209.

... if freedom is randomness, how can it be a characteristic of *will*? And ... What value or merit would there be in free choices if these were random actions which were not determined by the nature of the agent?

The general assumption underlying all those quotations is that the interrelated concepts of responsibility, chance, accident, and randomness[1] have a straightforward connection with the concept of necessary connection. It is assumed that necessary connection unequivocally implies responsibility and that the absence of necessary connection unequivocally implies chance or accident. Strangely enough, many who insist that the will is free are united in this same assumption with the Determinists whom they think they oppose. When we act responsibly and freely, we must, they think, act from necessity: but this necessity is of a supernatural or transcendent kind which frees us from the necessary order of natural events.[2] They frequently combine this with the belief that the supernatural influence is without exception a moral one: and that leads to the curious consequence that we are responsible for our actions when we do what is right but never when we do what is wrong. Again the assumption that responsibility is unequivocally identical with necessary connection explains why certain Libertarians (including myself when I first considered the problem) seek for a *tertium quid* between Determinism and Indeterminism in the idea of autonomy or self-determinism. They treat necessary connection as in some cases reflexive. This solution has also been adopted by non-Libertarians of the Hegelian kind as a *tertium quid* between Libertarianism and Determinism. Obviously then it has conflicting interpretations. One alone of these has to my mind any sense. On this interpretation self-determinism is simply equivalent to a form of indeterminism,[3] and accordingly its status as a *tertium quid* is destroyed.

In the chapters to come I shall show two things, or rather, the negative and positive aspect of the same thing:

(*a*) that the sense in which the agent is responsible for his voluntary action is not the sense in which we undoubtedly

---

[1] Cf. also R. E. Hobart, 'Freewill as Involving Determinism and inconceivable without it', *Mind*, January 1924; and P. H. Nowell-Smith, *Ethics*, pp. 281-2.

[2] Cf. Kant, *Fundamental Principles of the Metaphysic of Ethics* (ed. Abbot), p. 87.

[3] My grounds for this judgment are contained in Chapters VII and IX.

regard one of two necessarily connected events as thereby responsible for the other;

(b) that Libertarian indeterminacy is indeed incompatible with one kind of responsibility, but that it is equivalent to, as well as compatible with, the kind of responsibility peculiar to agents.

Given the negative conclusion (a) by itself, one could always reinstate the paradox which it appears to resolve. Even if two senses of the words 'responsible', etc., have been confused in one formulation of the paradox, the confusion might conceal a real paradox. Perhaps the responsibility peculiar to voluntary actions entails the deterministic type of responsibility for these actions. I remove this possibility in Chapter VII where I show that Libertarian indeterminacy is implied by (i.e. is an indispensable condition of) responsibility of the former type. This may provoke the awkward question 'What, then, are the other conditions for this type of responsibility?' Accordingly, in Chapter IX I go on to show that Libertarian indeterminacy is a sufficient as well as an indispensable condition of the former responsibility — and thus draw conclusion (b).

I come to the first or negative conclusion (a) in Chapters II to IV by showing that

(1) in principle the agent can be wholly or completely responsible for his action even where factors external to him are indispensable causal conditions of the action;

(2) necessary connection is a symmetrical and timeless relation, whereas the relation of responsibility between agent and action is asymmetrical and temporal.

In what follows I shall describe the type of responsibility which is equivalent to necessary connection between events as the 'explanatory' type, and the kind peculiar to the agent as the 'narrative' type. These descriptions may seem perhaps to take my conclusions for granted but are used for the sake of brevity alone.

CHAPTER II

EXPLANATION, ASCRIPTION, AND NARRATION

Two reasons for making a distinction between two kinds of responsibility have just been adumbrated in Chapter I. According to the first of these the agent can in principle be wholly or completely responsible for his action even where factors external to him are indispensable causal conditions of the action. It would seem to follow from this that even if the agent is wholly responsible for an action he need not be its sufficient causal condition (supposing for the sake of the argument that it has a sufficient causal condition). Now if there were only one sort of responsibility, a completely responsible agent would have to be a sufficient causal condition. Since, however, this consequence contradicts our conclusion, there must then be at least two sorts of responsibility. I elaborate the premiss of this inference and its implications more carefully in the rest of this chapter.

In the first section below I shall attend to a complicating factor. We shall see that, quite apart from a different sort of condition, no event or totality of events can be treated in an absolute sense as a *sufficient* causal condition for another. This may seem to destroy the antithesis which I am striving to draw between the responsibility peculiar to agents and events respectively. If neither agents nor events turn out to be capable of being sufficient conditions, there is no contrast between them in this respect. What is still more serious, the whole basis of the distinction in Chapter I between Determinism and Indeterminism may seem to be threatened. If events are necessarily connected in some way, it must be at least conceivable that some should be sufficient conditions of others. There is, however, a more restricted sense of 'sufficient' in which an event or totality of events can be legitimately said to be a sufficient causal condition of another. This is the main sense which I have been giving and will continue to give to the word outside the next section.

In the second section I shall go on to show that we can meaningfully attribute complete responsibility for an action to an agent. When we do so on any given occasion it is because we think that certain conditions have been fulfilled. The formulation of these conditions of complete responsibility will make plain that they definitely do not exclude the possibility that his action depends upon causal conditions external to the agent. Here, then, is one reason why the responsibility of the agent must be distinct from responsibility peculiar to causal conditions.

I

Even supposing the natural course of events is determined in accordance with laws down to the minutest detail, it remains true that the occurrence of no event or set of events is a sufficient condition in itself of the occurrence of any other event or set. To put the point more starkly let us consider everything that has happened in the universe at a given moment, though there may be limitations to the sense of such a hypothesis. Even this totality of events could not supply a sufficient condition whereby a later or earlier event or totality of events is determined in accordance with natural laws. To establish a sufficient condition we would have to add to the condition that each one of the totality has occurred the further condition that they all together constitute the totality of events, or equivalently, that there are no other events that have occurred at the same time.

Of course, even if the concept of the totality of events at a given moment is fully intelligible, it is something which only an omniscient being could hope to apply. Fortunately for the possibility of human science, however, there are relatively isolated systems of events which fall within our comprehension. Here again, however, any totality of events within a given period of time cannot serve as a sufficient condition for any event or set of events within the same system without the further proviso that the system is isolated and that no other event outside the totality is relevant.

Now, since the indispensable non-occurrence of other events is not the occurrence of an event, it would seem to be more accurate to regard the laws which govern the succession of events to be concerned with the necessary connections between facts about events. Most of these facts are particular facts that a given event or set has taken place: but before any conjunction of facts can constitute a sufficient condition of any other fact or conjunction of facts about events it must include a general fact which sets a limit to the range of particular facts. This conclusion follows from the formal structure of the scientific or causal laws[1] by means of which predictions or retrodictions are possible from the data given, and through which the necessary connections governing the occurrence of events are formulated.

By way of the simplest illustration let us take a scientific law of a relatively low degree of abstraction. According to the law of refraction from plane polished surfaces light is refracted at an angle equal to the angle of incidence. By means of this law we could predict with accuracy the point at which a beam of light will impinge upon a certain screen after refraction, *but only in the absence of certain conditions which are possible*. If some other refracting agent intervenes between the screen and the polished surface, or if the density of the medium through which the light is refracted becomes uneven, or if the screen disintegrates or moves within the period of time taken by the light to travel from source of emission to the position predicted, then the prediction will certainly not be borne out. The future will not be predictable purely in terms of the initial conditions specified, i.e. the angle of incidence and the position of the screen. It is even possible that the future will not be predictable solely in terms of the law or refraction but that other causal laws have to be called upon.

Altogether in making a prediction at any given moment about what will subsequently occur we must satisfy ourselves that two conditions are fulfilled:

(*a*) that the causal law or set of causal laws which we apply to the given situation is the sole law or set of causal laws to be applicable for the purpose of predicting;

(*b*) that if the law or set is the sole law or set applicable for this purpose to the situation, then it is applicable neither in a more nor in a less complex fashion than we allow.

In our example the screen might have shifted after the ray had been emitted and before it could strike the point predicted. Condition (*a*) will then be violated unless the predictor has realized that

---

[1] I use 'causal law' to indicate generally laws which govern the succession of events in more or less direct ways, though it can be used profitably to indicate a more specific type of law (cf. Mario Bunge, *Causality*, H.U.P., 1959, pp. 17ff).

other laws besides that of refraction are involved. On the other hand, the predictor may have allowed for the presence of only one plane polished surface between source of light and destination. The ray, however, may in actual fact be refracted by several surfaces before striking the screen. In such circumstances then, condition (b) will have been violated. The law of refraction is alone applicable to the situation, but in a more complex way than has been allowed.

Both conditions (a) and (b) must be held in mind, but in a perfectly unified science the fulfilment of (b) alone would suffice. A perfectly unified science is by definition a science in which only one law is applicable. In using such a law, however, it would be less easy to satisfy ourselves that (b) had in any given situation been fulfilled since it probably would be applicable in a more complex fashion than our incomplete knowledge of the situation would allow us to recognize. If, for instance, the phenomena of light were determinable in terms of laws governing the motions of particles, the laws of motion would suffice for predicting the point at which light would impinge on a moving screen, but only if we knew in detail the relative positions of all the particles out of which the ray, the refracting agents and the screen were composed.

The general principle from which both these conditions derive rather than their relative importance is, however, our more immediate concern. They provide for, by guarding against, the possibility that factors, additional to those which the prediction has taken into account, could by their presence prevent what otherwise would occur. They lay down, as an indispensable condition of the subsequent occurrence, that such factors should not in fact obtain.

There is one source of possible confusion that might conceivably obscure the truth of these conclusions. Quite apart from certain quantitative laws which can be regarded merely as definitions of physical concepts, many quantitative laws are at least partially analytic in structure. The quantitative ratios which they specify are logically contingent and verifiable or falsifiable by experience. On the other hand, the factors between which these quantitative ratios hold are analytically or logically correlative. It is logically conceivable for instance that the angle of refraction is not equal to the angle of incidence, but logically inconceivable that where refraction has taken place incidence has not taken place. The fact that in certain laws the analytically connected factors are successive, as in the instance of incidence and refraction, might possibly lead one to mistake the logically necessary connection for a causally necessary one. This would lead to the further mistake of supposing that the occurrence of a certain event could be in itself the sufficient condition of some other — that the occurrence of refraction, for instance, is not merely the logically sufficient condition of an antecedent incidence, but the causally sufficient condition as well. There are other laws, of course, where the analytically connected factors are not temporally successive. In Boyle's law, for instance, the analytically connected factors are the volume and the pressure of a gas. Anything with a volume can be considered as of logical necessity being under some pressure from zero upwards. Likewise, anything under pressure can be considered as of logical necessity having some volume. Once again it is the quantitative ratio between the two factors which is logically contingent. But there is not the same occasion for confusing the analytic connection with a causal connection, or of supposing that one event must under all conceivable circumstances be preceded or succeeded by another of a specific kind.

There is another argument in philosophical currency which purports to show that no event or group of events is a sufficient condition of another.[1] Unfortunately it is, to my mind, invalid. In concluding this section I cannot ignore it, because it bears a sufficient likeness to the argument which I have employed to make it a possible source of misunderstanding. It has been argued that if there is a discontinuity between cause and effect, then in the interval between the two there is always room for the intervention of other conditions. Consequently, the cause could never be the sufficient condition of the effect. If, on the other hand, cause and effect are conceived as continuous, the possibility of additional conditions that intervene is indeed removed, but, so it is argued, only at the cost of cause and effect becoming in part identical. Here the crucial issue is whether continuity does in fact entail

[1] Cf. A. E. Taylor, *Elements of Metaphysics*, pp. 171-4; Bertrand Russell, 'On the Notion of Cause', *Ar. Soc. Proc.*, *1912-13*, p. 7, reprinted in *Mysticism and Logic*; and R. G. Collingwood, 'On the So-called Idea of Causation', *Ar. Soc. Proc.*, pp. 96-8.

partial identity. To my mind it is only through an erroneous interpretation of a mathematical theory that one can suppose that it does. According to this theory, a line consists of a compact series of points, and a duration of a compact series of instants. 'Compact' is here understood in the technical sense to indicate that between any two points in the line, or any two instants in the duration, there exist respectively other points and instants. On this view of the constitution of a duration the instant that divides one segment of the duration from another must be part of both. If it belonged to a third, the two segments could not be continuous with each other. If, on the other hand, it belonged to one and not the other, then where does the other segment begin? At the next instant? But if the series of instants is compact, there can be no next instant. Other instants must intervene between the dividing instant and any other instant with which the segment that excludes the dividing instant is taken to begin. And consequently, once again, the two segments would not be continuous. Since this is contrary to our hypothesis, there can be no alternative to regarding the dividing instant as part of both segments. Let us now suppose that two segments of time divided by a given instant are exhaustively occupied by cause and effect respectively. If then the constituents of duration are instants in the mathematical sense, then the dividing instant must be part both of the cause and the effect, and cause must in part be identical with effect. And if, so the argument concludes, cause and effect are in part identical, then the cause is indeed a sufficient condition at least of that part of the effect with which it is identical: but it is a sufficient condition in the analytic sense of condition and not in the synthetic sense required by the relation between cause and effect.

The rejoinder to this argument is, however, obvious. A segment of time is not composed in any concrete or material sense of compact series of instants. These compact series are mathematical abstractions. The only sort of temporal unit which can either be separate or not from a second by a third is a finite segment of time. An instant is but the end of one segment of time and the beginning of another — no more a part of time or of either of the segments which it divides than a full stop is a word in either of two consecutive sentences. It isn't even what Russell has suggested[1] — a

[1] *Our Knowledge of the External World*, chap. v.

logical construct from events. Points and instants are not entities of any kind, otherwise one could ask at what points or instants they take place. Strictly they are or give positions rather than have position. Except in the indirect sense useful to the mathematician they are *neither* separated from each other by other instants *nor* contiguous. To describe a series of them as either compact or discrete is equally a category mistake.

In the concrete sense, then, the only sort of infinite divisibility into discrete parts which any finite temporal segment permits is, for instance, into series of non-overlapping segments of time vanishing towards zero. These are the segments to which the so-called compact series of instants give position. It does not follow, then, that two events, whether causally connected or not, are continuous only if the dividing segment is part of at least one of the two segments which it divides. Far less must we suppose, if we wish to maintain that the segments are continuous, that the instant belongs to both the segments which it divides.

The point of this argument which I have criticized seems to be that we never can enumerate all the particular causal conditions upon which a given event depends. Unless we make the actual beginning of the effect part of its causal conditions, an intermediate causal condition must always exist, or have time to exist, between any causal condition and the beginning of its effect. The point of the argument I have used, on the other hand, is that having enumerated all the particular conditions one has yet to stipulate as a *general* condition that there are no other particular conditions. Otherwise one has failed to specify the sufficient condition of the event's occurrence. The fact that there are no other particular conditions has nothing to do with the fact that there are no gaps in time between the particular causal conditions that have been enumerated and the effect. Even if there were no intervening gaps, there could be other factors which would prevent the occurrence of the effect. They might be partly or wholly simultaneous with the particular causal conditions enumerated.

Since no event or set of events can be a sufficient condition of others and in that sense completely responsible, the relation of necessary connection strictly speaking does not hold between events but between facts about events. The sufficient condition is composed of particular and general facts. Consequently I have

called the sort of responsibility which consists of necessary connection 'explanatory'; for explaining is the only thing one set of
facts can do or fail to do to another. This mode of description is,
however, not designed to deny an ontological basis to necessary
connection or that the connection holds between events. It is
merely intended to emphasize that it holds between events as
members of a system isolated in relevant respects from other
systems. Within such a system it is indeed permissible to describe
an event as a sufficient condition of another provided we do not
lose sight of the fact that it fulfils this function only as a constituent of a system. With this restriction in sense, then, one event
or set of events can legitimately be described as a sufficient causal
condition of another, and also, in the explanatory sense of 'responsible' as wholly or completely responsible.

2

There is, however, another sort of relationship which makes it
possible to say of one thing that it is wholly responsible for
another. It is logically possible to say of an agent that he is wholly
responsible for some particular action. This I take to be elementary, but there remains a question of interpretation which is not
quite elementary.

Professor H. L. A. Hart has suggested[1]

that the philosophical analysis of the concept of a human action
has been inadequate and confusing, at least in part because
sentences of the form 'He did it' have been traditionally regarded as primarily descriptive whereas their principal function
is what I venture to call *ascriptive*, being quite literally to
ascribe responsibility for actions much as the principal function
of sentences of the form 'This is his' is to ascribe rights in
property.

I agree that there is what might be called an ascriptive use of the
word 'responsible'. But underlying this use there is what I shall
call a narrative use of the same word. I use the word 'narrative' to
contrast this use with the explanatory use examined in the previous section as well as with the ascriptive use mentioned by Hart.

The following would I think be a fair summary of Hart's

[1] *Logic and Language* (ed. Flew), First Series, chap. VIII, p. 145.

article. 'Responsible' in the ascriptive sense means something like 'meriting good, bad, or indifferent treatment'. An agent in the ascriptive sense is responsible if he has some sort of merit positive or negative. But, and this is the novel point, this merit does not depend upon any definite characteristic of his action rather than another. To judge that an agent is responsible for something or that 'He did it' is, at the very least, to do more than make certain judgments about matters of fact. It is similar to the decision which a judge makes in the light of certain precedents. He is more often making law by creating a new precedent than merely acting in accordance with the existing law. By his decision he *makes* certain facts determine the issue. He doesn't merely judge that in the light of the existing law certain facts do without ambivalence determine the issue. He creates rather than interprets law. Likewise by ascribing responsibility to a particular agent one *makes* him responsible or creates his responsibility. One does this, of course, in the light of certain facts about his action, but in ascribing one chooses the sort of fact that will determine the issue.

I wish to show on the other hand that there is a non-ascriptive sense of 'responsible' or 'He did it'. There are ascriptive uses of these words as well, but the non-ascriptive use is presupposed by ascriptive uses. Certain facts about an action are relevant to its merit, and the relevance of some at least of these facts does *not* depend upon the choice of the person who ascribes merit. A non-ascriptive or 'narrative' type of responsibility depends upon this residual class of fact. We may notice this more clearly if we observe a very necessary distinction between two kinds of ascriptive responsibility: for each of the ascriptive kinds presupposes the narrative kind in a different way.

An agent may be wholly responsible in the ascriptive sense where he is the sole agent to whom any praise or blame for an action can pertain, even though he is not wholly responsible in the narrative sense for all its creditable or discreditable aspects. Thus in a railway disaster one may say of the signalman that he was wholly responsible for the accident in the ascriptive sense, where one merely wishes to exculpate some other person who has been involved, such as the engine-driver. One does not intend to deny thereby that the disaster was indeed an accident. One merely wishes to indicate, first, that the action of the signalman was one of the many voluntary actions that contributed to the accident, and second, that in its voluntary aspects it was the sole action of all the contributing actions that should not have been performed. Where the signalman's action may be presumed unintentional in its disastrous aspects, one does not, however, hold him guilty of murder but only of culpable homicide, if there are fatalities. Accordingly, a person can be wholly or partially responsible for an occurrence in the ascriptive sense without the stigma or credit being *moral*, if the occurrence taken as a whole was a fortuitous concatenation of actions, which taken in isolation from each other may each have been voluntary. The stigma or credit, or the absence of either, for the *voluntary* part of his action that led to the fortuitous whole will be, of course, of a moral kind: but it will at the same time be less than if the whole occurrence had been intentional.

In the instance of an accident responsibility, whole or partial, for the accidental occurrence is of the ascriptive kind alone. On the other hand an agent may be wholly responsible for an occurrence in both the ascriptive and narrative senses. When this happens the stigma, or credit, or absence of either, that pertains to the occurrence must be fully moral in character: that to which it pertains is in its possibly creditable or discreditable aspects a voluntary action of the agent through and through. Accordingly, what distinguishes the first kind of ascriptive responsibility from the second is this. Complete responsibility of the first ascriptive kind for an action in certain aspects implies only partial responsibility of the narrative kind for the action in the same aspects. Complete responsibility of the second ascriptive kind, on the other hand, implies complete responsibility of the narrative kind in precisely the same aspects. Both kinds of ascriptive responsibility, however, presupposes some degree of narrative responsibility.

In the instance of the railway accident, the signalman could not have ascriptive responsibility for it of the first non-moral kind, unless the occurrence had been in certain of its aspects an *entirely* voluntary action of his. At the same time, since it is an accident. it cannot in all its aspects be an entirely voluntary action of his. It may have comprised his absence from the signal-controls, and only if this was voluntary can he be held ascriptively responsible in the first way for the accident. But although he can be held wholly responsible for the accident in the first ascriptive sense (provided there has been no lapse on the part of other officials involved), he can only be held partially responsible in the narrative sense. And if his absence from the controls was entirely involuntary, due for instance to an unpredictable stroke, it is unlikely that he could reasonably be held responsible for the accident in any ascriptive sense whatever. He certainly could not be held responsible, whether wholly or partially, for the accident in the narrative sense, and consequently not in the second or moral ascriptive sense. The only sense in which he could be held responsible for the accident at all is the explanatory sense dealt with in the previous section, because his absence from the controls is a causal condition of the accident.

In making, then, the necessary differentiation between two kinds of ascriptive responsibility we have revealed the presence and to a certain extent the properties of an underlying narrative kind. The narrative kind is exactly coextensive with the voluntary whereas the general ascriptive kind is wider. Both the words 'responsible' and 'voluntary' derive their principal utility from the fact that the verb 'act' and 'do' have sometimes a narrow but more often a wider sense. In the more frequent and wider use they signify involuntary as well as voluntary behaviour. Even inanimate objects are said to *do* things or to *act*. In this sense these words and the words for particular actions (e.g. 'approach') have a quasi-narrative or purely descriptive sense. The relevant behaviour can be specified in purely ostensive terms. But some actions are voluntary, and when we refer to them as such our discourse is narrative as well as descriptive. 'I sprang to the saddle and Jorrick and He' is, for instance, the first line of a narrative and not merely a descriptive poem. We frequently use the word 'responsible' as well as 'voluntary' to make clear the distinction between the two kinds of discourse.

If an action is voluntary in all its ostensive aspects, then an agent is wholly responsible for the action in the narrative sense. If, on the other hand, it is only voluntary in some of its ostensive aspects, then the agent whose action it is can be only partially responsible for it in the narrative sense. The ostensive specifications give no indication of what might well be considered the most important fact about the action, viz. whether it is voluntary, and what persons are responsible, and the degree to which they are responsible. The railway disaster can be specified in ostensive terms but this leaves unsaid that it is a accident or fortuitous con-catenation of the behaviour of a number of agents, i.e. that it is involuntary. It further leaves unsaid, that one of the contributing factors in the fortuitous concatenation, viz. the signalman's be-haviour, was at the same time completely voluntary, an action for which he was wholly responsible.

Obviously, then, to complete our discussion and support these distinctions between kinds of responsibility, we must ask what makes an action voluntary. Two conditions are sufficient:

(*a*) the action must not be contrary to the agent's intentions;
(*b*) the fact that it is not contrary to the agent's intention must be at least an indispensable condition of its successful per-formance.

On these conditions I think both Libertarians and their adver-saries could agree. They are sufficiently liberal to recognize as voluntary such normally unreflective actions as breathing and blinking, or spontaneous, or impulsive actions, which some would feel disinclined to call intentional since they are unreflec-tive. At the same time they recognize the voluntariness of deli-berate or reflective actions as well. Superficially, however, they may seem insufficient for two reasons that I can think of.

First: can they decide the voluntary status of actions prompted by post-hypnotic suggestion? While in a hypnotic trance one may be told to perform a particular action so many minutes after regaining normal consciousness. One may, for instance, have been ordered to open a window, and in many cases when the allotted time comes round one does in fact open the window, probably thinking one is just satisfying a passing whim or even perhaps that one wants fresh air. Now is this action voluntary? Certainly the two conditions seem fulfilled. The action was not contrary to one's intention — one even was aware of an intention to do it. Likewise, the fact of the action not being contrary to the agent's intention is an indispensable condition of its performance. If one hadn't wanted to open the window one wouldn't have opened it.

To my mind the action really is voluntary. It is only as the obedience to a suggestion that it can be considered involuntary,

c

for it might be contrary to the agent's intention (damaging to his pride, for instance) to obey a post-hypnotic suggestion. But in fact one can say this sort of thing about many of our more normal actions which we wouldn't hesitate to call voluntary actions. Many of our actions are suggested to us and for reasons of vanity we might never have performed them if we had been aware of the fact. Indeed, only on the rarest of occasions are we spontaneously aware of all the opportunities for action afforded by our circumstances. And, in any given instance, it is almost as rare for us to realize that the action was suggested. What makes post-hypnotic suggestion unique is not its covert character so much as the method employed. Now we have already seen that any action may be (most are) voluntary in some respects and involuntary in others. In the instance of an agent unwittingly following out a suggestion, the action suggested can be involuntary only when considered as obedience to the suggestion.

To point to the important role of unrecognized suggestion in action may, however, seem damaging to Libertarianism. Does it not upset the metaphysical neutrality I have so far tried to observe? But why should the Libertarian deny the truism that an agent is more likely voluntarily to realize a project which he entertains than one which he does not entertain? And why should he not admit that there are limits to the agent's ability to conceive action spontaneously? The agent's intelligence, education, general knowledge, and social contacts can without hesitation be recognized as controlling what enters into the agent's mind. Having admitted all this the Libertarian can still maintain with perfect consistency that it remains causally unsettled whether the agent will aim at the end which he entertains. Of course, in the instance of post-hypnotic suggestion it seems that the agent having entertained the suggested project is more likely to realize it than not. But it is quite easy to explain this tendency as a voluntary one. When one finds one gives more attention to a trivial project than it seems to merit the rational thing to do is to be rid of it by realizing it in action, in the same way as one gives in to a nagging wife for the sake of peace.

A second reason for making reservations about the sufficiency of our two criteria of voluntariness may be found in what are called 'compulsions'. Is the child who sucks his thumb, the kleptomaniac, the sex-criminal, or the miser behaving voluntarily? Again by our two criteria they may seem to be. Can we not say that these people know what they are doing, very often intend to do it, or in any case do not at the operative moment intend not to do it, and also that if they had intended not to do it they would not have done it? Yet we may feel doubts about calling such actions voluntary.

The reasons for hesitation are obvious. Compulsive actions are incongruous or inappropriate. We feel inclined to say that the agent really does not know what he is about even when, as above, we felt compelled to admit that he is aware of the bare facts about his action. Compulsive action violates the first criterion in rather a curious way. It is not contrary to the agent's intention as a result of any sort of external force. Neither is he, in one sense, ignorant of the nature and circumstances of his action. In one sense he knows very well what he is about to do and, afterwards, what he has done. What he is unaware of is his *real* intention. And there is no need to jeer at the word 'real' here. What it indicates is quite clear. The action is inappropriate not because the agent is ignorant of what it and the objects round about him are. It is not like aiming a rifle which one mistakenly takes to be unloaded, or like sitting on a chair that isn't there. The action is inappropriate because the agent is unaware of what these objects are *not*. They conceal because they are confused in his mind with other objects.

This concealment seems to be what in psycho-analytical theory is referred to as symbolization. The thumb symbolizes the mother's teat because subjectively speaking that is what it 'conceals'. But we needn't underwrite psycho-analytical theory in all details. Take for instance the miser whose behaviour displays the incongruity typical of compulsion. What does his money conceal from him?

One account is that it conceals or symbolizes his faeces, but let us consider an alternative, viz. that it conceals his personal inviolability. Inviolability is indeed less palpable than faeces, but possibly more relevant. In fact it may account for the infantile concern for faeces which when unwisely interfered with leads to traumatic conditions. Under the pressure of our environment, particularly of our social requiremnets, a more sensitive differentiation of our aims or ends may become necessary. In the process of this differentiation the individual may become confused. His life may lose its integrity — his ends their essential unity. Instead of his new life being a development through differentiation of the old he may feel that it has little continuity with the latter and no longer any self-consistency. The miser retains an integrity or inviolability of a rather stunted form.[1]

Now personal inviolability is the sort of end which we may have of necessity. This necessity, however, is not a deterministic psychological sort of necessity. Personal inviolability is the sort of end that may underlie, or precondition, most, or all, of our more specific ends. The necessity is of a logical kind. There is an inconsistency about not willing one's personal inviolability analogous to the inconsistency, mentioned by Kant, of not willing the development of one's talents. Since one's talents qualify one for the successful execution of one's aims one cannot consistently will their atrophy. Likewise, short of willing suicide of character, the preservation of the personality which we express in our particular actions is necessarily willed in the willing of these actions

On this analysis we can see why the miser's behaviour becomes compulsive. An end, which he need not choose from logical or any other kind of necessity, comes to symbolize or conceal an end which by logical necessity he must choose. In this way the former acquires a spurious sort of logical necessity so long as the agent fails clearly to see what it is not. It is this spurious logical necessity that exercises the compulsion. The miser knows what his money is, but he does not know that it is *only* money. If he knew that his money was not his personal inviolability he would be in a position to stop or to continue hoarding, and simultaneously to pursue or change his main or general purpose. If he does not stop hoarding, then probably his hoarding was voluntary, i.e. consistent with his intentions, all along. If, on the other hand, he does stop hoarding, then probably, other things being equal, his hoarding was involuntary, i.e. inconsistent with his intentions, all along. Other things, of course, might not be equal. He might continue hoarding for an entirely new set of reasons, such as an unprecedented instability in stocks and shares. Accordingly, his new rational behaviour might obscure the fact that his previous behaviour had taken an irrational form, which, other things being equal,

[1] Cf. François Mauriac's *Le nœud de vipères*.

would have ceased as soon as he discovered what his money is not.

I wouldn't like to say whether this spurious sort of logical necessity is an essential ingredient of all compulsions. The most I need to maintain is that objects of compulsive desires 'conceal' ends which are fundamental to human nature whatever that means. It is likely, however, that the process of symbolization, whereby secondary objects such as thumbs and money come to stand for or 'conceal' more primitive objects such as teats or faeces, arises from the fact that these primitive objects specify at a certain age-level more general and comprehensive ends, which should take other and more complex specific forms at later age-levels. Personal inviolability is an example of this general sort of end. Security is another. In early years the child may not possess the conceptual capacity to distinguish the specific from the general aspect and this may explain why the traumatic experiences which give rise to compulsions are most commonly the earliest. It also suggests that psycho-analytic methods which don't probe beyond these primitive objects may remove the compulsion, but tend to perpetuate the infantile traits in the patient by persuading him that they are fundamental.

What alone is germane to my main argument in this analysis, however, is the part which suffices to show that compulsive behaviour, contrary to first appearances, does not conform to the first part of our criterion of voluntariness, viz. that voluntary action cannot be contrary to the agent's intention. We only feel doubt on this matter if we fail to distinguish between ignorance of what one's action is and ignorance for what it is not. In its positive aspect the agent's compulsive behaviour is not inconsistent with the first part of our criterion but in its negative aspect it is.

For these reasons, then, the two conditions of voluntariness can stand as sufficient despite the apparent difficulties. Now whether an occurrence is not contrary to the agent's intention, and whether its not being contrary is an indispensable condition of its occurring, are both matters of fact rather than matters of ascription. This is true whichever of two dominant interpretations of statements about intention one cares to adopt. They may be categorical statements about mental occurrences, or alternatively, they may be reducible to hypothetical statements or 'mongrel-categorical' statements about such publicly observable events as what the agent would have done in certain circumstances.[1] I don't wish to suggest that one must adopt one or other of these views, but merely to point out that on either, the presence of an intention is not a matter of ascription. In Chapter VII I shall try to give a more adequate analysis of intention than either of these, but this will leave unaffected our present conclusion that matters of intention are non-ascriptive.

We have seen, then, in the first part of this chapter that the relation of necessary connection is strictly speaking a relation between facts about events, or alternatively between events only as constituents of a system. No event or set of events can be wholly responsible for the fact that another event or set has occurred, since the sufficient condition consists of general as well as particular facts about events. It consists of the composite fact that certain events have occurred and that no other events of relevance have occurred. In the second part of this chapter we have seen, on the other hand, that the agent can have complete responsibility for his actions. Since, then, the agent is a person and not a set of particular or general facts, one might argue that there must be a distinction between the two sorts of responsibility I have labelled 'explanatory' and 'narrative'.

I have, however, just conceded that an event can be regarded as a sufficient condition of another, subject to its interpretation as a constituent of a system. Why, then, shouldn't the agent be regarded as a sufficient condition of his action subject to the same sort of restriction? Two answers to this have emerged from the last section.

(1) Even supposing an agent could be conceived as a sufficient condition in the restricted sense of his action, he wouldn't necessarily be wholly responsible in the manner typical of agents; for the action might be involuntary. The two conditions of voluntariness have first to be fulfilled for there to be responsibility of the relevant kind. If, then, the agent is wholly responsible for an act in this way, it is only by being a sufficient condition of a specific sort. Hence, for this reason if for no other we must

[1] G. Ryle, *The Concept of Mind*, pp. 138ff.

distinguish other forms of responsibility from those belonging to sufficient conditions as such.

(2) However, it is clear enough that the agent can be wholly responsible for an action in the manner which is typical of agents without being the sufficient condition of the action at all. The conditions of voluntariness lay it down that the absence of contrary intentions must be an indispensable condition of the action. But in many cases of action other conditions are indispensable to the action besides the absence of contrary intentions. Since these are frequently of an environmental nature and external not only to the agent's mental states but also to his body, the agent cannot be the sufficient condition. I don't wish to imply by this that the agent as such is some sort of condition of his action, but merely that if one tries to regard him as any sort of condition one has to concede in many cases the presence of external or environmental conditions which are just as indispensable to the action as the conditions that can be identified with the agent.

For these considerations we must distinguish a narrative from an explanatory form of responsibility. If we don't we can, of course, adopt the expedient of finding the agent responsible not for his action, where that depends on environmental conditions, but solely for some sort of effort to act or do. Professor C. A. Campbell, for instance, attributes[1] moral responsibility to the agent solely for exercising some sort of moral effort rather than for the successful conclusion of moral effort. His grounds are that the agent must be the sole source of that for which he is morally responsible. But people *do* things: they don't merely *try* to do them: and it is with the analysis of responsibility as efficacy or the doing of things done that we are concerned. When I turn off the air-conditioner it is I who stop it, not I and, say, the disconnecting action of the switch except in a distinctly miscegenated sense of 'stop'.

While, then, events must always fall short of being sufficient conditions in the unrestricted sense, the agent, in so far as he can be correctly identified with a condition at all, must always fall short of being a sufficient condition in the restricted sense. Hence, the responsibility typical of the agent can in no sense be identified with the necessary connection between events. We have also seen

[1] *Selfhood and Godhood* (Allen & Unwin), p. 168.

why we must distinguish between the narrative and ascriptive kinds, the latter of which for similar reasons must also be distinguished from the explanatory kind. The distinctions in responsibility recognized by the chapter as a whole can be exhibited as follows:

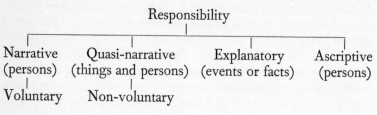

This method of division is of course without prejudice to relations of dependence between the co-ordinate subdivisions. Thus the ascriptive kinds presuppose the properties of an underlying narrative kind. There is as well the apparent possibility that the narrative kind of responsibility, while distinct, might yet be reducible to the explanatory type. In later chapters I shall argue that narrative responsibility, or voluntary action, is indeed reducible to necessary connections between events, but not to the one-one necessary connections postulated by Determinists.

CHAPTER III

AGENT, SUBSTANCE, AND EVENT

A SECOND reason for distinguishing an explanatory from a narrative type of responsibility is to be found in the property of symmetry.

I

The one-one necessary connection between events which Determinists postulate is, in the first place, symmetrical. On the other hand, the relation between an agent and his voluntary action is asymmetrical: the agent does the action, but the action does not in the same sense do the agent — the action is not responsible for the agent in the same sense as he is responsible for his action.

This contrast is often obscured by our use of such terms as 'cause', 'effect', 'necessitating' or 'determining' to express relations of necessary connection. They suggest that the relation between effect and cause, necessitated and necessitator, or, what is determined and what determines may not be the same as the converse relation. On the other hand, the laws of those branches of science such as classical mechanics from which Determinists are wont to draw their model of the universe express the necessary connections which govern the sequence of events in the form of equations. Now equality is a symmetrical relation. Consequently the necessary connection expressed in equations fails to display the asymmetry which the distinction between cause and effect seems to require. Possibly the term 'law', however, has further misleading implications. It might suggest the presence of a legislator who by some sort of exertion compels phenomena to behave consistently with these equations; or at least it might suggest the presence of an exerted force, if the idea of a legislator is rejected as too metaphysical. The laws are held to state the principles in accordance with which such forces as gravity, magnetism, etc., are exerted, in somewhat the same way as civil laws state the principles in accordance with which political force is exerted.[1] But the

---

[1] Cf. Schopenhauer, *The Fourfold Root of the Principle of Sufficient Reason* (Buhn's Philosophical Library), p. 51.

literal interpretation of such terminology has very little support among modern scientists. Even seventeenth-century scientists like Galileo and Newton, who were tempted to interpret force literally as a physical concept, don't give this interpretation whole-hearted support. They distinguish with care the necessary connections of phenomena, which they expressed in scientific generalizations or principles, from the occult agencies which they postulated to explain these connections. Quite explicitly they abstain from speculation about such agencies on the grounds that they are beyond the province of experimental science.[1] Consequently, experimental science is not even concerned with an asymmetrical relation between force and phenomena.

To accept the literal implications of such terms as 'law', 'force', etc., when applied to physical phenomena is evidently to assimilate physical phenomena to human actions and to ignore the important differences between the direct relation of agent to voluntary action, on the one hand, and that of event to event on the other.

The asymmetry required by such terms as 'causing', 'necessitating', 'determining', etc., might of course, be found in the asymmetry of temporal relation between one event and the successor in time with which it is necessarily connected. Thus the fact that incidence of light at a particular angle *precedes* refraction at the same angle, makes one identify the incidence with the cause which necessitates, or determines, refraction at the same angle as its effect. But the fact that there are other relations between the values of this particular equation, and that these relations happen to be asymmetrical, does not make the necessary connection between them likewise asymmetrical.

One might, of course, define responsibility not solely in terms of necessary connection but in terms of temporal antecedence as well. In that case the responsibility of one event for another would be as asymmetrical as the responsibility of an agent for his voluntary actions. Nevertheless, the asymmetry must have a different source in either case. This we can see if we turn to the contrary concept of chance. When discussing the necessary connections between events it is as significant to say that A^1 rather than A^2

[1] Cf. Galileo, *Two New Sciences* (New York, Macmillan, 1914), pp. 166-7 and 293; Newton, *Principia* (tr. Cajori), pp. 546-7; and Mortimer Taube, *Causation, Freedom and Determinism*, pp. 113ff, for a discussion of these and other passages.

preceded B^1 'by chance' as to say that B^1 rather than B^2 followed A^1 'by chance' using in both cases the same senses of 'chance'. On the other hand it is not significant to say that a certain action had a particular agent 'by chance' in the same sense of 'chance' as it is significant to say that he did a particular action 'by chance'.

Suppose one says 'Sir Alexander Fleming discovered penicilium quite by chance'. This means something rather different from 'It was quite by chance that it was Sir Alexander Fleming who discovered penicilium'. Possibly the first statement gives support to the second, but whereas it represents the discovery of a substance with the properties of penicilium as not having been its discoverer's specific aim, the second states that there were other discoverers who might as easily have discovered it. This second statement could conceivably be false, say on the grounds that Sir Alexander was the only investigator to be pursuing a line of research likely to lead to his 'chance' discovery, while at the same time leaving it open that he made it by chance. To say that a particular action has had a particular agent by chance is simply to aver the equal likelihood previous to its performance of its having been performed by somebody else.

Since, then, a particular action cannot have a particular agent by chance in the same sense as is usual when we say that an agent performs an action by chance, it follows that chance in the latter sense consists of an asymmetrical relation. In this sense alone it is correlative to by excluding 'narrative' responsibility, but not correlative to the 'explanatory' type. Hence the same asymmetry must also belong to responsibility of the narrative kind but not of the explanatory kind. I shall describe this asymmetry more positively later in this chapter.

There is, indeed, another kind of asymmetry or, more accurately, nonsymmetry between events in one-one necessary connection, or the values of different variables in a causal law. Furthermore, this nonsymmetry, unlike temporal antecedence, does depend upon the necessary connection. It has, however, a purely epistemological origin, and is not essential to necessary connection. One event can be said to *determine* and the other to be *determined*, when the first gives us the value of a variable in the scientific formula by means of which *we* can determine, i.e. compute, specifically what the other event must be without actually needing to observe the latter. By calculation we determine *what* this latter event is: we do not determine *that* it is what it is — we do not cause it. Similarly, it is our *conclusion* that the latter is what it is, which is necessitated by the *premise* that the former is what it is.

Now whether we use the earlier of two successive events rather than the later in order to determine the other, depends upon which is given and which is not. If the earlier event provides the data we predict the later event; and if the later event provides the data we retrodict the earlier event. A scientific formula can be used for either purpose: the nonsymmetry of this kind of determining depends purely on the accident of what we know.[1]

Obviously this nonsymmetry is quite distinct from the temporal asymmetry of antecedence. It is, furthermore, still less capable of accounting for the asymmetry of the agent's responsibility for voluntary action. Voluntary action cannot be responsible for agents in the same sense as agents are responsible for voluntary actions.

We must, of course, admit that certain forms of necessary connection are asymmetrical. Necessary connection may be many-one or one-many as well as one-one. I have only shown that the necessary connection between events, which we designate by 'cause', etc., and 'effect', etc., respectively, may be symmetrical. Consequently any asymmetry that justifies the use of these terms must belong to additional relations between events and not to necessary connection as such. We must note too that if the asymmetry of responsibility were to be found solely to consist of the one-manyness or many-oneness of given instances of necessary connection our initial question how responsibility is compatible with indeterminacy would disappear. The question is profitable just because there is a sense in which responsibility is incompatible with indeterminacy. Hence we cannot trace the asymmetry of responsibility in that sense to any indeterminacy in the events for which the agent is held responsible.

The historical reasons why we use asymmetrical terminology for expressing symmetrical relations of necessary connection must be omitted from this discussion. R. G. Collingwood has

[1] Cf. A. E. Taylor, *Elements of Metaphysics*, p. 175; B. Russell, op. cit., *Ar. Soc. Proc.*, p. 15.

contributed valuably[1] to this subject, but there is much in his interpretation of the facts with which I disagree.

2

The relation of an agent to what he does voluntarily is that of a substance to an event, and therefore manifestly asymmetrical. It would be distinctly odd to say that what he has done is responsible for the agent for this reason alone — at least if one were to use 'responsible' in the same sense as when one says the agent is responsible for what he does voluntarily. Perhaps, however, I should try and remove any possibility of the point I am making at the moment being misunderstood for one which I am about to make later on. For the moment I am merely distinguishing between two kinds of relationship, i.e. the explanatory and the narrative type of responsibility, while neither affirming nor denying that the one type may be reducible to another. Determinists could agree that the narrative type is substance-event in form and at the same time maintain that the explanatory one-one event-event relation is its logical condition. For instance, they might say that when an agent is responsible for his action in the narrative sense his volition of the action is responsible for his action in the explanatory sense, and then add that preceding events are likewise responsible for his volition in the explanatory sense. Narrative responsibility on this account would be reducible to a subclass of explanatory responsibility. At the moment, however, I wish merely to guard against the confusion of one of the two types with the other.

C. D. Broad has provided an instructive instance of this confusion. He believes that a Libertarian interpretation alone can recognize the presuppositions of our ethical judgments, i.e. our belief in what he calls 'categorical obligability'. On the other hand, he believes that indeterminacy is not a sufficient condition of categorical obligability. We wish to hold the agent responsible for doing, among the actions which indeterminacy makes possible, that particular action which he did in fact do rather than any of

---

[1] 'On the So-called Idea of Causation', *Ar. Soc. Proc.*, *1936-37*, pp. 96-8. In its least misleading use it seems that the word 'cause' should be restricted to that limited part of the total particular conditions of an event which is controllable relative to a particular agent. Since in this sense it presupposes agency there is, of course, no possibility of the word being so used in the analysis of agency or responsibility of the narrative kind.

the others. Broad believes that this responsibility is a condition additional to indeterminacy, and gives the following account of the way in which he thinks Libertarians might try to recognize what he believes:[1]

> I suspect that they would quarrel with my statement that on their view, the fact that one puts forth such and such an effort in support of a certain desire is, in the strictest sense, an accident. They would like to say that the putting forth of a certain amount of effort in a certain direction at a certain time *is* completely determined *by the agent or self* considered as a substance or continuant, and not by a total cause which contains as factors *events in* and dispositions of the agent. If this could be maintained, our puttings-forth of effort would be completely determined, but their causes would neither be events nor contain events as cause factors. Certain series of events would then originate from causal progenitors which are continuants and not events. Since the first event in such a series would be completely determined, it would not be an accident. And, since the total cause of such an event would not be an event and would not contain an event as a cause factor, the two alternatives 'completely determined' and 'partially determined' would both be inapplicable to it. For these alternatives apply only to events.

Of this supposed defence he observes:[2]

> Now it is surely quite evident that if the beginning of a certain process at a certain time is determined at all, its total cause must contain as an essential factor another event or process which enters into the moment from which the determined event issues. I see no *prima facie* objection to there being events that are not completely determined. But in so far as an event is determined, an essential factor in the total cause must be other events. How could an event possibly be determined to happen at a certain date if its total cause contained no factor to which the notion of date has any application? And how can the notion of date have any application to anything that is not an event?

[1] *Determinism, Indeterminism, and Libertarianism* (C.U.P., 1934), pp. 42-3, reprinted in *Ethics and the History of Philosophy*.
[2] Op. cit., pp. 44-5.

Both Broad and his Libertarians have failed to realize that the substance-event type of responsibility belongs to a totally different category from the event-event type — for the former type is not causal at all. The difference is not merely in the category of one of the terms, viz. the referent of the relation. The two types of relation themselves belong to a different category. This has been obscured by taking the statement that the agent is responsible for his action as synonymous with the statement that the agent determines his action. When the word 'determine' is used in this way with an accusative rather than with an infinitive, as in 'determine to do', it normally expresses a relation of the explanatory kind which holds between events and not between a substance and an event. Broad, of course, has used the term 'accident' in these passages and not the correlative term 'responsible'. But if there are two kinds of responsibility there are likewise two kinds of accident which one must be careful to distinguish. The solution, then, to the alleged Libertarian dilemma is not that the agent's action is no accident, since it is determined by a continuant or substance, i.e. the agent. The relation of determination can only hold between events. On the contrary, the agent's action is no accident, in the one relevant sense of 'accident', because his action is a voluntary one for which he is responsible in the relevant sense of 'responsible'. Perhaps the failure to distinguish the event-event type from the substance-event type of relation explains also why Broad and his Libertarians interpolate these 'puttings-forth' of effort between the agent and his action. Their motive may be to postpone to the very last moment the anomalous necessary connection of a substance to an event, and if one postulates an occult type of event, the queerness of its necessary connection to a substance may be less apparent.

Broad can still object that even if an explanatory type of responsibility is distinguishable from a narrative type, nevertheless the antecedents of an action should provide a complete explanation of why the action occurs at one date rather than another. But this is exactly what the Libertarian indeterminacy defined in Chapter 1 does. It denies that every specific event has a *sufficient* antecedent causal condition, but not that it has an *indispensable* causal condition. Now as long as an event has the latter, even though it has not the former, there is an absolutely sufficient explanation of its temporal position. One must not confuse the explanation of temporal position with the explanation of why it rather than a limited number of other events should occupy that particular temporal position. Libertarianism witholds this latter explanation alone.

One argument of a rather insidious kind remains against the substance-event interpretation of action. Broad suspects[1] that Libertarians who underwrite it may have been misled by a certain quite normal looseness in the use of the word 'cause'. Where a stone breaks a window it is not uncommon to say that the stone is the cause and the broken window or the breaking of the window the effect. Apparently, then, the causal relationship has in this instance been identified with a substance-event relationship. But, of course, to say that the stone is the cause is only a loose way of saying that the stone coming into contact at a certain velocity is the cause of the breaking of the window. The causal relationship is really an event-event relationship and not a substance-event relationship at all. The same will apply to persons. We say, for instance, 'He was the cause of all the trouble'. Even in voluntary action, then, there is according to this argument no genuine substance-event relationship.

Broad himself, however, has been seduced by the same loose use of 'cause', though in a rather different way. It explains why he has assumed without question that the substance-event relationship is a causal relationship. The looseness which leads to a causal relationship between two events being described as a substance-event relationship may have led him to assume that all substance-event relationships are causal. Plainly they are not, as even the history of the same stone is enough to show. Even in the loose sense we never say that the stone is the cause of its flying through the air. Yet the stone in flying is doing something, viz. flying. It has efficacy.

It is possible, of course, to split the flight of the stone into constituent flights, and possible, perhaps, to describe each antecedent constituent as the cause of the subsequent one. But this move is not required to explain why we call the stone the cause of its flight for the simple reason that we never call it the cause of its flight. In any case to split an event up into causally related consecutive parts can only postpone the realization that every event,

[1] Op. cit., p. 45.

composite or incomposite, is normally described as something being done by something in the category of substance. The most we can do is to reduce a particular application of the substance-event relation to an event-event relation. We cannot eliminate the category itself unless we go a step beyond ordinary usage and patronize more technical categories such as sense-data or White-head's four-dimensional physical object-events which have been designed specifically for the purpose of eliminating substance.

A clear distinction between substance-event and event-event relations is, however, no better than a preliminary to the under-standing of voluntary action or narrative responsibility. Other substances besides persons, and persons as well, are commonly regarded as performing actions which are of a non-voluntary sort. Hence the substance-event asymmetry is not a unique mark of the specific form of narrative responsibility we are trying to characterize. We might, of course, prefer to call the responsibility of sticks and stones 'quasi-narrative' since narratives are peculiarly concerned with people in their voluntary actions rather than with things. So long, however, as the way in which quasi-narrative stops short of true narrative responsibility is left unexplained it still may seem possible that the substance-event relation has very little to do with what is peculiar to the latter alone.

D

CHAPTER IV

ACTION AND PROCESS

To appreciate fully that the relation between a substance and an event belongs to a different category from the relation between an event and an event we have to attend to something more than its asymmetry. Asymmetry alone has merely marked the difference in category between the *referents* of the two types of relation. The more important distinction is between the timeless and temporal characteristics peculiar to the explanatory and narrative types of responsibility respectively. Indeed, we cannot fully understand the categories of substance and action until we have fully understood this further distinction. A general misunderstanding explains the disrepute which has in recent years attended the category of substance and the consequent misunderstanding of action. Substances are things with histories, i.e. a past and possibly a future. Actions constitute these histories. To put it more formally, substances are subjects of verbs for which tense distinctions are significant. An understanding of the distinction between what has been done by the agent and what he is about to do is indispensable to an understanding both of doing and the agent.

I

The relation of necessary connection is a formal timeless relation between events. It is not a material temporal occurrent relation: it is not the kind of relation of which events consist: it only holds between events. On the other hand the relation of narrative responsibility does constitute events if we regard actions as a class of events. It is the relation between the doer and what he does.

Laws of nature can be treated[1] as analogous to the rules of logical inference. When we assert that p implies q where p and q are propositions, we assert something the truth of which is independent of time. The tense of 'implies' is the timeless or logical present. Now when applied to events, the word 'cause' can be

[1] Cf. Carnap, *Philosophy and Logical Syntax*, chap. II, para. 5.

used in this respect in exactly the same way to connote a propositional operation.[1] The rules of this kind of operation must, of
course, vary in certain respects from those of implication. Like
'implies' we can use the word 'cause' to connect two propositions
p and q when they refer positively or negatively to certain events
as having occurred, occurring or about to occur. When used in
this way it expresses with perfect adequacy the relation between
events which the causal terminology of more ordinary speech is
meant to indicate — provided we observe the conditions laid
down in Chapter II. The sufficiency of p as a causal ground for
inferring q must always be taken as relative to some causal law or
set of laws. Consequently p is the sufficient ground for the inference under the two conditions that

(*a*) the causal law or set of laws which we take as applicable to
the given situation is the sole causal law or set of laws applicable
for the purpose of inference;
(*b*) if the law or set be the sole law or set applicable, it is applicable neither in a more, nor in a less complex fashion than we
allow.

When 'causes' is used in this way, however, we must remember
to observe the same distinction between validity and truth which
we observe in logic. If we say that p implies q, we imply in this
usage neither that p nor that q is true. On the other hand, causal
terminology frequently carries the suggestion that the things
which are causally related are facts, or actual events, or things
that do exist. To say 'Something causes interference in my television set' is to suggest both that the something is factual, and
that the interference has taken place, or will take place by causal
necessity. The tense of 'causes' is here the habitual and not the
timeless present. The correct interpretation of tense, of course,
depends very much on the context of the statement. In 'A car-
engine causes interference in a television set' it is more likely that
the tense of 'causes' is the timeless and not the habitual present.
Whether it is the habitual rather than the timeless present depends
upon how far one can accurately substitute 'is causing' for 'causes'
in the proposition.

[1] Cf. Arthur W. Burks, 'The Logic of Causal Propositions', *Mind*, vol. LX, No. 23,
July 1951.

In contrast with the verb 'to cause' the use of the word 'to imply' can never imply that, where the ground refers in the affirmative to an occurrence, the occurrence must be actual. The truth of p implies q implies the truth neither of p nor of q. The fact that 'to imply' can be used in other tenses than the present might indeed obscure this. These other tenses, however, have the function of limiting the applicability of the rule of inference to some particular period of time. I might say 'In my day bad health implied financial ruin' without strictly implying that during the stated period anybody's health was bad. Although it is unlikely that everybody enjoyed good health at that time, my statement could be based not upon instances but upon the fact that there were no health insurance schemes in being then. Consequently, the whole statement is convertible to the timeless present with no loss of meaning, as distinct from elegance, simply by putting ground and consequent in propositional form somewhat as follows: 'That X's health was bad before such-and-such a date implies that X was financially ruined.'

Those facts of usage can then be summed up in three conclusions:

(1) There are instances where the use of the verb 'to cause' is very similar to that of 'to imply'. In whatever tense we use the verb, we can translate the sense without any substantial loss of meaning by asserting that one proposition *is* the sufficient causal ground for inferring another proposition, where 'is' is in the timeless present.

(2) Where this conversion is possible the existence of nothing whether substantive or occurrent is being implied.

(3) There are, however, instances where the use of the verb 'to cause' is less closely parallel to the use of the verb 'to imply', for the existence of some substantive or occurrent is implied.

Because of this third conclusion I may seem to have shown no more than that the necessary connection expressed by 'cause' is *sometimes* of a purely formal and timeless kind. What I engaged to show was, on the other hand, that it is *always* of a formal and timeless kind. But we must accept this stronger conclusion. Otherwise, we would have to deny that one event causes another only because they satisfy a valid causal law. Accordingly, when the verb 'to cause' is used with existential implications it must express something more than the necessity of connection between occurrents. The additional implication, however, is not that the necessity between the connected events is something material as distinct from formal. When we say that one event has caused another we are not describing the occurrence of some occult output of energy in addition to the two events, even though we imply that these two have taken place.

To treat the causal relation as material would lead to paradox. In addition to a first-order series of events that cause, and are caused, e.g. the running of a car-engine, we would require a second-order series of events, viz. the causings exercised and suffered by the first-order series. The event which is the running of the car-engine would have to stand to the process of causing interference in the same sort of substantive relation as the car-engine stands to the process of running. Consequently, we would require a second-order time-dimension within which the first-order event could persist as a substantive or continuant, in the same way as the first-order substantive, e.g. the car-engine, persists in the first-order time-dimension throughout various activities such as running. Furthermore, is there any reason why second-order events should not persist and cause in a third-order time-dimension in the same way in which first-order events were required to persist and cause in a second-order time-dimension? Likewise is there any reason why the regress should stop at the third-order time-dimension, and not continue to infinity?

Now, this regress or possible regress may seem worth while to some as a speculative hypothesis. It is not, however, an intended implication of the ordinary use of the terms 'cause', 'effect', etc. If we say that the forced march of Blücher caused the tide of battle to turn against Napoleon at Waterloo, it is not our intention to attribute an independent history to this forced march in addition to the history of Europe of which it forms a part. When we say 'Europe was unsettled then' we may either be comparing or contrasting the state of Europe then with what it is now or will be at some time in the future. But in saying that Blücher's forced march 'caused' we are not conceding that at some date later than 1815 the relation it held then to Napoleon's defeat may possibly change to something quite new. The past tense of the verb 'to cause' is meant to indicate merely the time of the march and the defeat relative to the present. The causal relation between the events is treated as unchanging.

We may conclude then that when causal terminology is used to indicate necessary connections between events the relation it describes is formal and timeless. Also we may note that the analogy with the use of the word 'imply' justifies further my description of this usage as explanatory.

2

A full explanation of the precise manner in which the agent-action relation contrasts with the formal timeless relation of necessary connection between events will be the work of several chapters. Only the first steps can be taken here. The distinction is one between a relation which one event may bear to another and a relation which constitutes these events as events.

There are in fact two ways in which we can regard anything which takes time. We can treat it either as a unit or as a unity. These two ways, of course, are not mutually exclusive. When we treat the event as a unit we treat it as externally related to other events antecedent, concurrent, or subsequent. When, on the other hand, we treat it as a unity we are attending to its internal structure. Obviously we can attend to its internal and external relations at the same time. Now when we treat it as a unity there are two further ways in which we may regard it. We may regard it as made up of smaller externally related units, or we may regard it as what I shall call 'a process'. When we treat it as a process we treat it as composed of stages of development — and stages in the same process are not externally related to each other. They include and overlap each other. Bound up with the notion of stages and development there are, of course, the further notions of potentiality and actuality. The earlier stages are potentially the later stages and the later stages are the actuality of the earlier stages.

This distinction can perhaps be elucidated by the following somewhat crude diagram:

T^1 T^2 T^3 T^4

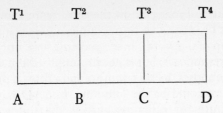

A B C D

The superscripted forms of the letter T here represent successive instants in time, and the line which they punctuate at equal intervals a similarly punctuated stretch of time, e.g. the period from Monday to Thursday morning. The letters A to D represent the limits of specific events or processes, e.g. a leisurely journey up the Malay peninsula with Singapore, Kuala Lumpur, Ipoh, and Penang as the successive points of arrival or departure on each morning or evening respectively.

When we conceive this journey as consisting of event-units we represent it as the sum of AB, BC, and CD in temporal order or otherwise. When on the other hand we represent it as a *process*, we represent it as consisting of AB, AC, and AD in that order. Each of the latter three events is represented as a separate stage in the final stage, i.e. the completed process AD: alternatively, each is regarded as a form complete or incomplete, actual or potential, of AD. I shall show that when we treat a temporal unity as a process, we regard the earlier event-units as in one-many necessary connection with the later ones. Thus, given CD, the preceding events BC and AB must be given by necessity, since in accordance with the one-many pattern they are indispensable conditions of CD. In the same way BC must presuppose AB. But neither the occurrence of AB nor the occurrence of BC presupposes respectively the later occurrence of BC and CD. Each later event accordingly sums up the earlier event.

One way of giving AD this sort of structure is simply to regard AB as the first of its components, BC as the second, and CD as the third. We would have to describe the journey up country in this way. Instead of saying we did the journey in three stages, viz. Singapore to Kuala Lumpur, Singapore to Ipoh, and finally Singapore to Penang, we would surely say that on the first day we went from Singapore to Kuala Lumpur, on the second from

Kuala Lumpur to Ipoh, and on the third from Ipoh to Penang. Here the task of successive aggregation of events into stages in a process falls upon the words 'first', 'second', and 'third'. By definition a third presupposes, but is not presupposed by, a second; and a second presupposes, but is not presupposed by, a first, since the first component could be the only one. But AD might have the process structure for other reasons as the following example shows.

Let us take the temporal whole consisting of a stone breaking a window. This is represented as a process if it is considered first as the stone coming into contact with the window, and then as the stone breaking the window, since the parts are articulated as stages and not as mutually exclusive. If, on the other hand, it is represented as consisting first of the stone coming into contact with the window, and then of the *window* breaking, then it is represented as a whole consisting of events, because the parts are mutually exclusive. Observe here how the second event-unit, i.e. the *window* breaking, presupposes, but is not presupposed by, the earlier as soon as it is *described as* the stone breaking the window. The earlier event-unit, i.e. the stone coming into contact with the window, does not presuppose the occurrence of the second, since other causal conditions might conceivably intervene to prevent the latter (cf. Chapter II). Here, then, a one-many structure has been imposed upon the temporal unity by the definitions of the terms used to describe it. We could, of course, change it to a one-one structure by describing the stone's coming into contact with the window as the stone's being about to break the window. In this way the window would be broken by definition. However, it may not be broken in fact. We have to wait until it is broken before we can describe the preceding event in that way. In contrast we can describe the second event as soon as it occurs, in such a way as to presuppose the first since, of course, the first has already occurred.

This explains in a preliminary way how we can distinguish relations holding between events from relations which constitute events. Unfortunately, it must give the impression that relations between events are fundamental to relations which constitute events, since I have defined the second in terms of the first. This would lead to an infinite regress since by definition a constitutive relation must be more fundamental than a relation holding between events thus constituted. I cannot remove these regressive implications until Chapter IX. In the meantime we must attend as a necessary preliminary to certain refinements in our notion of process.

CHAPTER V

TYPES OF PROCESS

THE task of locating the type of process peculiar to voluntary actions or actions for which the agent has genuine narrative responsibility still lies ahead. To this end we must refine the notion of process further. I shall now propose and explain a number of broad distinctions mainly in order of expository convenience.

   (i) Activities and Phenomena.
  (ii) Self-determining and Non-self-determining Processes.
 (iii) Prospective and Retrospective Processes.

As principles of division these pairs are not mutually exclusive. Some of them can be used for subdividing the division made by others. More important still, however, is that some are more fundamental than others. In particular we shall in later chapters use the third distinction between prospective and retrospective process to explain more fully what distinguishes voluntary from non-voluntary activities.

Activities and Phenomena — What distinguishes an activity from a phenomenon in the sense in which I use these words is simply that an activity is a process expressed by a verb the subject of which is a substance whereas a phenomenon is a process expressed not by means of a verb but by means of a substantive. In many cases the distinction is merely at a verbal level. When we talk about countries declaring war, persons behaving or misbehaving in various ways, organisms growing or decaying, and inanimate objects moving or interacting, we are describing activities in my sense of the word, since I am also interpreting the category of substance sufficiently liberally to include all these different sorts of entity. Activities, then, are phases in the history of substances. There are, however, other process-describing sentences in which the substantive expression does not refer to a substance. It refers to a complete process, e.g. 'the Reformation', 'the Second World War', 'the Edinburgh Festival', the 'sunset', 'the blast of a foghorn', 'the whine of a siren', etc. The events to which the first three of these expressions refer could no doubt be described by sentences which refer to the behaviour of individual substances. The Edinburgh Festival, for instance, consists of the behaviour of individual artists and the members of their audience. On the other hand, the latter three expressions seem to refer to sensations, or, to use a more specialized term, sensa, as distinct from physical objects. No doubt they contain references to substances, but the inadequacy of our vocabulary for referring to sensa except by reference to the material objects with which they are associated is a familiar one. When we refer to a sunset, or to the blast of a foghorn, or to the whine of a siren, we are not necessarily alluding respectively to the sun setting, or a foghorn blowing, or a siren whining, nor in general to the activities of a substance.

What distinguishes a phenomenon decisively from a substance is the verb of which it may be the subject. These verbs all belong to the second order. They do not describe processes in the way in which activity verbs do. Their function may be to express causal relationships as in 'The war has caused a shortage in rubber supplies' or 'The throbbing pain keeps me awake at night'. Alternatively they may describe stages in the completion of a process, its duration, location, or extent. Thus we may speak of the Edinburgh Festival lasting three weeks, of the Italian Renaissance beginning, spreading or gathering momentum, etc., and of the last Olympic Games having been held in Sydney. It can be seen that the verbs used here do not narrate the history of anything in the same way as activity verbs. Instead they relate activities to spatio-temporal co-ordinates. When we turn to the subject of prospective process we shall pay particular attention to one specific set of co-ordinating expressions, viz. 'present', 'past', and 'future'. These adjectives are used to indicate stages in a process in a special way and tense inflections perform the same function in a parallel manner.

The main point of distinguishing activities from phenomena is to guard against confusion between two different functions of verbs associated with process. This particular form of confusion might not lead to serious error but could blunt our appreciation of the significance of process. In most cases it is perhaps better to express the distinction at the purely verbal level using the formal

mode of speech, since most processes can be described in either
way. The existence of sensations and more controversially of
sense-data constitute an exception, since they are independent of
substance in important senses. If one is phenomenonistically inclined one will wish to reduce all statements about activities to
statements about the sensum-class of phenomena and maintain
that the latter are more basic and elementary. This is an issue
which I wish for the moment to leave open.

Self-determining and Non-self-determining Processes — An example of a non-self-determining process has already been put to
considerable use, and its main features should by this time be
sufficiently familiar. When a stone breaks a window the event
which we describe in this way is organized by our mode of
description into a temporal unity. We could easily, however,
choose a mode of description in terms of which the content of
this unity would become bifurcated or even more complexly
fragmented. According to my interest I can view what has occurred as the stone breaking the window, or the stone coming into
contact with the window and the window breaking.

These are alternative methods of grouping the content of
what falls within one particular strand of time or spatio-tem-
porally continuous region. They are not equivalent, for only if I
regard what has occurred within these limits as one process, viz.
as the stone breaking the window, would I regard the stone
coming into contact with the window as a preliminary stage, viz.
as the stone being about to break the window. According to the
one way I make a distinction between the preliminary and final
stages, and according to the other I distinguish between complete
and self-contained processes. Which of the two alternative
methods of organization I adopt need depend only upon the
subjective factors of my interest and attention. The content alone
may be objective and independent of these.

What is true of the stone is in fact true for all processes what-
soever. The way in which we identify and delimit what happens
need depend, in its organization though not in its objective content, solely upon our interest and attention even where what
happens is organized independently of these as well. Viewed in
this way all processes can be regarded as non-self-determining,
for the organization is dependent upon the person who describes

them. Even the voluntary actions of an agent may be viewed in this way, at least by others, or by the agent himself with the spectator's eye. Travelling to a destination can be considered picaresquely as a number of self-contained journeys, or as one which takes place in several stages. In fact there is no illuminating difference under the category of non-self-determining process between voluntary and non-voluntary process.

In contrast, where a process is self-determining there are objective reasons in addition to subjective ones for attending to just one particular section of time and space, and for taking it as a temporal unity. We are objectively justified in regarding a specific grouping of event-units as a temporal unity where the relatively later event-units determine the relatively earlier event-units, but not vice versa. Let AD be the temporal unity of which the event-units are in necessary connection. Then, it is only if CD is the sufficient condition of BC and AB, and BC the sufficient condition of AB, and furthermore, if neither AB is the sufficient condition of BC or CD, nor BC a sufficient condition of CD, that there are objective reasons for regarding AB as a stage in AC and AC as a stage in AD. If, on the other hand, each of the three event-units were a sufficient condition of all, it would be perfectly legitimate to regard AB as a stage in AC, and AC as a stage in AD. Each of these stages is certainly an incomplete form of AD, but they are not stages in the development of AD as a *necessarily connected* whole. They are not stages in the objective determination of AD as an objectively determined whole. The objective determination of the whole would be as complete in AB as in AD. Likewise, if the earlier stages alone are sufficient conditions of the later, they cannot be stages in the objective determination of the whole, because the whole would be completely determined at the beginning instead of at the end alone.

In supposing that necessary connections may be asymmetrical I am not, incidentally, going back on Chapter III. We saw that asymmetry does characterize one-many or many-one necessary connection. Likewise when I say that one event may be a sufficient condition of another, I am not going back on Chapter I. Its sufficiency must be understood as relative to the two conditions that were outlined.

In finding examples of self-determining processes I am under no obligation to vouch for these examples being genuine, since their function is purely illustrative. Consequently I shall be treading on no deterministic toes by giving instances where later events determine earlier but not vice versa. However, even supposing that genuine examples can be given, they are possibly reconcilable with deterministic premisses. Successive events which are in strictly one-one necessary relationships in their more determinate characteristics may in their more general characteristics display one-many necessary relationships, if indeed they display any at all.

One type of change which apparently exemplifies self-determination is that of organic growth (or decay). In the classic example of the growth of an oak tree from an acorn one can reasonbly assert that unless there is an acorn, there will be no oak, and, accordingly, that if there is an oak, there must have been an acorn. On the other hand, there is plenty of evidence to show that acorns may not develop into oak trees. Conditions of soil, weather, etc., are all equally indispensable to the growth of an oak. We may note in passing, however, that this asymmetry of necessary connection between acorns and oak is perfectly compatible with the symmetry of Determinism. The presence of an acorn is an element which a number of incompatible total situations might have in common. Accordingly, the apparent indeterminacy in the consequences of this common element could be explained deterministically in terms of the variety of additional factors that differentiate from each other the various incompatible situations in all of which the acorn is present.

It is not entirely irrelevant to notice a further feature of organic growth. It illustrates a distinction between temporally definite and temporally indefinite process which is of incidental interest to the discussion of ends in Chapter VIII, Section 1. I refer to the plasticity[1] displayed in the growth of organisms by which the final characteristic may be achieved in any one of a number of ways. To take an extremely simple instance, the acorn will in suitable conditions grow into an oak tree whichever way it is planted in the ground. If planted with the germinating part downwards, the shoots will very soon turn round and strike upwards. Because of this we ascribe to organic behaviour a teleological or quasi-teleo-

---

[1] Cf. R. B. Braithwaite, *Scientific Explanation*, p. 329ff, who, however, makes no adequate distinction between this and the self-determining characteristic of organisms.

logical character: the organism behaves as if it were adopting a means to a specific end. Now, in consequence of this adaptability the organic process is within limits a temporally indefinite one, since the length of time for its completion will depend upon the presence or absence of snags which it has to surmount.

In illustration of temporally definite self-determining characteristics we can turn to the field of history. It is plausible to suppose that a certain historical event, either in its specific or general characteristics would never have occurred if it had not been preceded by another particular event, and that particular event alone. At the same time it would be less plausible to claim that given the antecedent event the subsequent event followed inevitably. We would regard the latter claim as far more ambitious than the former. Now one of the things we might expect the historian to explain is why the historical process in question took the length of time it actually did take to reach completion. We might ask him why it took Germany so long to achieve nationhood as compared with neighbouring states. In actual practice, of course, we would not expect him to explain the duration of the process within very exact limits. It might not even be possible to assign exact temporal limits to the process in question. But nevertheless, allowing for a certain margin of inexactitude, we do expect explanations of the duration occupied by a process from the historian, as well as explanations of why the process happened at all. Accordingly, we may regard historical processes as illustrating the temporally definite type of self-determining process.

These illustrations, however, have only limited value. We saw how processes of the non-self-determining kinds are in a manner subjectively conditioned not in content but in organization. To a lesser degree this is true also for the self-determining processes which I have used as illustrations. They exhibit one-many necessary relationships in respect of characteristics which are rather general and our selection of these features rather than more specific ones is determined by subjective interest. The growth of the acorn has the one-many relationship to the growth of the oak tree only with respect to these rather general characteristics which I am mentioning now. If, however, I were able to describe an instance of the sequence of these two events more specifically, or just differently, the connection might for all that has been shown to the contrary turn out to be one-one. It will follow of course that where the specific as well as the general characteristics of a series of events displays a one-many pattern of connection then this structure is not subjectively conditioned, at least not in the present sense. Later we shall see that this type of process could be described as subjectively conditioned in an entirely different sense. So far as actions are conditioned by intentions they are subjectively conditioned and such actions are in fundamentals specifically self-determining processes. I mention this here only to avoid the possibility of later confusion.

The need arises now to distinguish between two kinds of self-determining process, and here for the first time we come to the fundamental distinction between processes, or the doer-doing relation on the one hand, and event-event relations, on the other. So far we have supposed that, when considering what occurs within a particular spatio-temporal area as a process, we are taking events in an order of increasing inclusiveness instead of one after another. But since events are processes, this manner of elucidation has had the disadvantage of analysing process in terms of itself. All we have really succeeded in doing so far is to show the relation of a comprehensive process to its distinguishable sub-processes. In actual fact, however, we have hit upon the essential characteristic of a process or event, viz. the one-many relation of dependence holding between its parts. While we dealt with subjectively conditioned processes it was possible to regard the constituent events as independent entities, which we could view separately or together according to the way in which they affect our interests. Actually, however, what constitutes an event as an event is the fact that it occupies a place as a term in a one-many relationship of dependence. The subjectively conditioned processes are simply processes which display a one-many structure in the interdependence of their parts which is additional to the structure which actually constitutes these parts as events. The proof of this is given in Chapter ix.

Prospective and Retrospective Process — A distinction of this sort becomes necessary if we are to understand the various ways in which, to use Aristotelian categories, the later stages in a process are potentially in the earlier, and can be said to be their actualities. It is a paradox in the Aristotelian system, accentuated no doubt by latinized translation, that his actualities need never become actual. The acorn sometimes 'fails' to become an oak. Similarly the traveller who has reached Ipoh on the second evening of a three-day journey up the Malay peninsula, is not thereby entitled to say quite literally that he will reach Penang the next evening. In the interim his car may break down, or he may be recalled to Singapore, or he may just become fed up. Of all the things that might happen his arrival next evening in Penang is, of course, by definition of terms the most appropriate if one chooses to describe his successive arrivals and departures on previous days as stages in the journey from Singapore to Penang. But it is important to realize that one has full warrant to describe it in this way only *after* the three-day period has elapsed and the journey been completed. Hence one may describe this sort of process as retrospective.

If the full period elapses without his arrival in Penang, one can, of course, continue to describe the earlier arrivals and departures as stages in the process of completing the journey simply by describing the journey as abortive. This manner of speech, however, if taken quite literally as applicable to all processes, may lead to the impression that nature is being frustrated in some way, and to a belief in some true actuality that lies latent not merely in persons in the form of their intentions but in things like stones and acorns which commonly are held to be incapable of intending. One can avoid this conclusion if one realizes that in grouping together as a process a set of events which could as accurately have been described as discrete one is adopting a retrospective outlook. The fact that some of the events may be anticipated and may not in fact occur does not gainsay this, for a retrospective outlook may be anticipated as well.

In prospective process on the other hand the actuality to which the preliminary stages point is the actuality which is about to occur quite literally. Where a later event is the actuality of an earlier event it must occur. This kind of 'aboutness' is the kind possessed by anything in respect of its future. But we must notice here an important distinction between what *was*, what *is* and what *will be* about, or going to, happen. Something that *is* about to happen must happen. On the other hand, something that *was* about to happen or *will be* about to happen may not have hap-

E

pened, or may not happen, respectively. Thus one can say 'The train was about to depart when at the last moment the guard caused a delay'. Or again 'He will be about to depart, and then you must prevent him'. But one cannot correctly say 'This is about to happen, but something will prevent it', although one can say 'This is about to happen, if nothing happens to prevent it'. If something really is going to happen then by definition nothing can prevent it.

These differences between retrospective and prospective process are not differences of content. One and the same process can be considered as retrospective or prospective. The stages of any process that has taken place must have had in the moments of their occurrence prospective potentiality. The distinction between the stages of prospective process is simply the distinction which we make when using the terms 'past', 'present' or 'future', and the equivalent tenses or temporal adverbs. The present consists of the pastness of one set of events and the futurity of another. The past is the incomplete actuality and the future is the completion of what the past is potentially. Unlike the past and the future, then, the present is not a period of time but a date at which two adjacent periods of time are respectively in the past and future. As such it is not to be contrasted with the past and the future considered as periods of time, but, on the contrary, with dates in the past and future when the distinction between past and future was or will be different.

On this interpretation, then, the present corresponds say to the point C at T^3 in the diagram. The past would then correspond to AC between T^1 and T^3, and the future to CD between T^3 and T^4. The contrast between C on the one hand, and B on the other, would then be between the date when AC and CD *are* in the past and future respectively, and the date when AB and BD *were* respectively in the past and future. Again, the contrast between C on the one hand, and D on the other, would be between the date when AC and CD *are* in the past and future respectively, and the date when AD, and whatever follows outside this end of the diagram, *will be* respectively in the past and future. To treat C rather than B or D as the present is simply to treat it as the date which dates B or D as past or future dates. These dates of course date C in turn but only in the indirect way in which a past or future date can date the present.

This interpretation of the present as a date is, of course, essential to the elucidation of the idea of prospective process, and I propose to show that it is unequivocally supported by the facts of linguistic usage. We do, it must be admitted, speak in certain circumstances of 'in the present' just as we speak of 'in the past' of 'in the future'. This might mislead one to suppose that the present is a period of time correlative to the past and future rather than the date of the past and future. But, on the other hand, while common usage allows us to say 'at present' it does not allow us to say 'at past' or 'at future'; and this is sufficient to establish the dating function of the present relative to the past or future. The phrase 'in the present' has a more complex purpose than may first appear, and I shall discuss it later.

Let us first see what would happen if we did not interpret the use of the terms 'past', 'present', or 'future' in the way I have indicated. There will be two other possibilities.

According to the first, an event might be past, present, or future, in the way in which one geometrical figure may be smaller, equal to, or greater in area than another. Of these three relations both *smaller than* and *greater than* allow many different sizes of figure as their referents, whereas equal to allows only one size of figure. This analogy might explain why 'the present' seems to refer to something much narrower than either 'the past' or 'the future'. The analogy holds in other important respects as well. No two of these three geometrical properties can consistently be attributed to the same figure at the same time. Likewise no event can at the same time be past, present, and future or any two of these.

There, however, the analogy stops. The same two geometrical figures must at all times be related by the same relation of size. It is not only inconsistent to say at T^1 'A is both smaller and greater in area than B'. It is likewise inconsistent to say at T^1 'A is smaller in area than B' and then at T^2 'A is greater in area than B' (provided that by definition of terms no change in the area of either figure is permitted). On the other hand, as McTaggart pointed out,[1] it may be necessary to say at T^1 'A is in the future' and at T^2 'A is in the past', although, of course, it would remain inconsistent to say either at T^1 or at T^2 'A is both in the past and the future'.

[1] *The Nature of Existence*, section 332.

The difference between the two types of sentence, one about area and the other about time, lies in the function of the copula 'is'. In the sentences about area there is no point in distinguishing the function of 'is' from the function of 'was' or of 'will be': this followed from the definition of 'the same figure'. In the group of sentences about events, the distinction between 'is', 'was', and 'will be' does have a useful and necessary function. In the sentences about area the copula is timeless: in those about events it is temporal. Now the temporal copulae indicate that the sentences in which they occur may only be true at the moment of utterance, which is from the utterer's point of view the present. Consequently, since adjectives like 'past' and 'future' can only occur in such sentences, their applicability must be relative to the present. This is the true explanation of the narrowness of the present relative to the past and the future. The analogy in narrowness between the present and the geometrical relation *equal to* was quite misleading.

These arguments dispose of the first method of regarding the present as correlative with the past and the future instead of as a date for the distinction between past and future; for they show that the truth of a statement about what is in past or future depends upon the statement's tense. But one might argue alternatively that though the present has this dating function along with past dates and future dates, it may be correlative to the past and future as well. One might take as evidence the fact that we sometimes use the phrase 'in the present' and not merely the phrase 'at present'. Since we also use the phrases 'in the past' and 'in the future', this might suggest that like 'past' and 'future' the word 'present' may indicate a period of time as well as a date. By referring to a period of time as 'the present', however, we don't necessarily treat it as correlative with the periods of time that are past and future. A thick black line on a sheet of paper is extended like the areas which it divides. Nevertheless, even when aware of the fact, we usually treat it as a limit, common to the two areas rather than as an intermediate area. Again, while aware of the size of the Pyrenees we usually treat them as the boundary between France and Spain and not as third country. Likewise, when we speak of a number of events, as in the present, we draw attention principally to the fact that they are temporal boundaries between the past and the future, even while recognizing that they have relative to each other a temporal order as well. If we want to ignore the reference to the past and future which these events limit, we have to invent a philosophical or psychological locution such as 'the specious present'.

However, let us suppose that the present is a correlative of the past and the future as well as a date, and see where this leads us. It will imply that the present not only dates the pastness or futurity of events, but also the presentness of other events as well. Not only will one contrast the distinction between past and future at present with past or future distinctions, but one will have to contrast the present at present with the present in the past and future. Now I feel a greater uneasiness about saying 'In 1815 the battle of Waterloo was in the present' than I would feel about saying 'In 1816 the battle of Waterloo was in the past' or 'In 1814 the battle of Waterloo was in the future'. I would feel inclined to put 'the present' in quotation marks while leaving 'the past' and 'the future' unadorned. Otherwise, to make the former statement, would be similar to saying 'In 1815 the battle of Waterloo was happening now': and this seems to suppose some odd kink in time whereby events of 1815 are identical with something occurring now. On the other hand, the corresponding versions of the latter two statements would be 'In 1816 the battle of Waterloo was no longer happening' and 'In 1814 the battle of Waterloo had not yet happened' respectively: and in contrast these two statements in no way outrage our sense of normality. Accordingly, normal usage suggests that the present is not correlative to the past or future, since the phrase 'in the present' does not occur in the same way as the phrases 'in the past' or 'in the future', nor the adverb 'now' in the same way as the adverbs 'no longer' or 'not yet'.

I do not suggest, however, that any logical absurdity is entailed by taking the present as a correlative of the past and future. I only maintain that as a matter of linguistic fact we don't, and further-more, that it is unnecessary and uneconomical to do so. The present, as we saw earlier, must have at the very least a dating function to prevent logical absurdities. Accordingly, if we make it a correlate of the past and future which it dates, we are involved in an infinite regress. We imply that the presentness of an event must be past, present, or future, in the same way in which the pastness of futurity of an event may be past, present, or future. But if this is so, then the second order past, present, or future must likewise be past, present, or future and so on *ad infinitum*. When discussing infinite regresses one must, of course, resist the temptation to call them 'vicious' by way of rhetorical flourish. I can see nothing vicious in this particular regress.[1] Vicious regresses are limited to regresses which arise from analysing concepts either directly or indirectly in terms of themselves; but no attempt has here been made to define anything.

The regress is objectionable here simply because it is unnecessary. In its place one can substitute an indefinite regress by confining the function of the present to that of dating instead of something that is dated. In functioning as a date the present is in contrast with yet other dates — a contrast between what is at the present in the past or future and what was in the past, or will be in the future, in the past or in the future. These other dates, however, since they are all in what at present is the past and future, must all be dated by the present as well. But one can in addition, *if one wishes*, date them by other dates than the present. When one uses the pluperfect tense, e.g. 'He has had a bad start in life', one places an event in what is past relative to a date which is in the past relative to one's present: likewise, when one uses the future perfect tense, e.g. 'We shall have left by then', one places an event in the past of a date which is in the future relative to one's present; and there are infinitely more of these indirect ways of locating an event in time than the grammarians have taken the trouble to recognize. So long, however, as one does not treat the present as correlative to, as well as dating, the past and future, there is no logical necessity that one should date dates as well as events.

It might be argued, however, that unless we suppose that the present functions as more than a date, we cannot account for the facts of experience. Without a third container, comparable to the past and future, would we have to omit certain events from our inventory of reality? Linguistic usage may seem to suggest this. We frequently use the adverbial 'now', or the adjectival 'present', to refer to periods of considerable length.[2] We even speak about

---

[1] McTaggart assumes without any argument that there is. (Loc. cit.)
[2] Cf. Findlay, 'Time: A Treatment of Some Puzzles' (*Logic and Language*: First Series, pp. 40ff.)

'the present epoch'. Where we use temporal inflections we not only say 'He did X' or 'He will do X' but also 'He does X' or 'He is doing X'. If the present is a date alone, must we cut out the events to which we allude in the present tense from the totality of existence? By no means. This use of the present tense is dictated purely by our method of describing occurrences. We might want to refer to an occurrence only as a member of a temporal unity, and if this temporal unity is sufficiently long in duration and insufficiently remote in the past or future it must straddle the point of division between the past and the future. But it is always possible to group occurrences in such a way that the grouping does not straddle the present, although it may be the straddling grouping alone that happens to interest us. Thus, while writing the previous sentences I might have answered the question 'What are you doing just now?' by saying 'Writing this sentence'; but, carefully synchronizing my speech with my pen, I might have said 'I have just written the word "although" '. It would of course be eccentric to answer the question in this way, because to ask the question at all implies that one is prepared to tolerate a margin of inaccuracy which is sufficient to accommodate the length of time during which one could reasonably expect a reply. To treat an event as a limit is, as I have already said, no more odd than to treat a mountain range or a river as a boundary between two countries.

The present, then, is a stage in prospective process or the process of time. It is distinguishable from past stages for it includes in the past what *was* previously in the future and excludes from the future some events that *were* previously in the future. It is likewise distinguishable from future stages because it excludes from the past some events that *will be* in the past and includes in the future some events which *will not be* in the future.

This completes my explanation of the distinction between retrospective and prospective process. It completes likewise the explanation of the distinction between relations that relate events but which are themselves timeless and relations which are temporal because they constitute events. Necessary connection is a timeless relation whereas the relation between potentiality and actuality is a temporal relation constituting process. It is natural at this point to raise the question whether the timeless type of relation is logically related in any way to the temporal type. Does one presuppose the other in any form? In Chapter VII I propose to show that the temporal relation does not presuppose one-one necessary connection of the deterministic type and in Chapter IX that one-many necessary connection of the Libertarian type entails the temporal type of relation. It will become obvious in these chapters that these issues depend very much upon whether retrospective process is the more ultimate type. Can prospective process be analysed in terms of the relation of inclusion and exclusion holding between temporally ordered aggregates of events, as our interim diagram seems to suggest, or is the idea of process basic to the idea of an event? I wish to leave these questions undecided for the moment.

It is important to understand that the three broad distinctions we have been investigating in this chapter have been distinctions between categories under which processes are subsumable rather than between species of process. The same process may in certain cases, though not in all, be subsumable under several of these. Certain of these categories are, however, more basic than others and in the course of sorting out their mutual relationships in the following chapters we shall solve the problem inherited from the previous one by finally locating voluntary action. What is the difference between the action of an object of any sort and the voluntary action of a person? An obvious but unambitious answer is that the presence of intention or purpose, or at the very least, the absence of any contrary intention or purpose, is indispensable where the action is voluntary. This answer, however, leaves the precise nature of intention or purpose undetermined. It does not explain specifically the precise part played by intention in the process-like structure of action.

At the moment two conceptions of intention seem dominant. Both of them lend themselves more directly to a deterministic interpretation of action than to Libertarianism. The more traditional account of the two interprets intending or purposing as mental events which are antecedent causal conditions of voluntary action. The less traditional account gives a dispositional analysis in the Rylean manner.[1] Thus to say that an action is

---

[1] *Concept of Mind*, pp. 138ff.

voluntary is interpreted as shorthand for a number of statements, all but one of which are essentially hypothetical in form. Ryle calls this analysis 'mongrel-categorical'. For instance 'X caught the 9.30 a.m. intentionally' would be the equivalent of 'X caught the 9.30 a.m. and if he had been given the wrong platform number and hadn't discovered the error in time he would have missed his train, and if he had slept in he would have hurried to catch it ... ' On either of these accounts, then, the relationship of responsibility is reducible to a one-one, or, at least, to a many-one necessary connection between events. Libertarians, on the other hand, postulate one-many necessary connections. Accordingly, they couldn't regard responsibility for voluntary action as consisting solely of the intentionality of the action as analysed in either of these two ways. If an intention is an event with only one action as its possible overt effect, then they would have to postulate an indeterminacy amount the agent's intentions. If, on the other hand, Ryle's mongrel-categorical analysis of intention is correct, they would have to suppose that the causal condition of the truth of the categorical statement (e.g. 'X caught the train') has itself no sufficient causal condition but falls within a range of indeterminacy.

In the next chapters I propose to show that neither of these two accounts of intention are adequate. Many of the issues, accordingly, between Libertarians and Determinists have been misconceived. No account of intention is adequate which cannot give adequate recognition to the agent's standpoint towards his voluntary action at the moment of performance. From this standpoint voluntary action falls under the heading of prospective process in a way which is compatible neither with the dualistic interpretation of an intention as a mental event nor with the mongrel-categorical analysis.

CHAPTER VI

INTENDING AND PREDICTING

INTENTIONS or purposes as we have seen in Chapter II are involved positively or negatively in voluntary action as such. Now intentions belong to the type of thing which language can express. They are expressed in categorical predictions of the form 'I am going to ... ', or 'I am about to ... ', or 'I shall ... ' In the course of the next two chapters I shall show how, through understanding the logic of expressions of intentions, we can discover the essential difference between the voluntary actions of persons, on the one hand, and their non-voluntary actions, or the actions of things other than persons on the other.

By the word 'prediction' I refer simply to a statement about the future irrespective of how it is backed by evidence or even whether or not it is meant to be supportable by evidence. Because of their categorical form predictions which express purpose have the characteristic tendentiousness or comparative lack of warrant which distinguishes any statement about the future from equally categorical statements about the past. Categorical predictions, of course, are frequently warranted by inductive generalizations derived from past experience. But their warrant is only that of a conclusion based upon data and never as strong as the warrant of the data. The warrant of any conclusion inductive or deductive is indeed, weaker than the warrant of the premises particularly since inference may be faulty. Predictions, however, owe their tendentiousness not to the fact (when it is a fact) that they are conclusions. It is truer to say they are conclusions (when they are conclusions) instead of data, because of an essential lack of immediate warrant due to their not yet having been verified by experience.

Where we deal specifically with predictions that express purpose, their tendentiousness quite clearly is of an even more radical kind, which, indeed, makes it misleading to look upon them as conclusions at all, even while distinguishing them from mere guesses. The action which the agent intends to do seems to depend at least in part, unless it happens coincidentally, upon the agent's intention to do it. But since his prediction that he is going to do it is the vehicle of his intention, his intention can hardly enter into his calculations as apart of the data upon which his prediction is based.[1] Therefore, since the data are *ex hypothesi* incomplete as conditions apart from his intention, his prediction must in principle have even far less warrant than any other sort of prediction. There is an essential lack of the mediate or inductive sort of warrant to which all other types of prediction are amenable. The data for guesses about the future, for instance, are incomplete in fact but not in principle.

This argument, of course, rests on the assumption that intentions really are expressed most appropriately in the form of a specific categorical prediction, and further, that as well as having this *form* they actually *are* categorical predictions, or imply facts about the future. Since the conclusion which I have just based on this assumption has potent ontological implications of an indeterministic sort, the presupposition must be subjected to careful scrutiny. In the rest of this chapter I shall demonstrate what everybody nowadays seems willing enough to concede, viz. that the form is categorically predictive. The task is not otiose, however, because in the process implications which this unanimity has tended to blur will become more definite. In the next chapter I shall show that expressions of purpose are predictive in substance as well as in form at the same time as considering the ontological implications of this conclusion.

To show that the form 'I am going to ... ' expresses purpose, and to make further the necessary modifications to this claim, let us consider several sets of contrasted expressions. Each group will include at least one expression of this form. The first is the triad

(1) 'I am going to sneeze'
(2) 'I am going to sleep'
(3) 'I am going to catch the 9.30 a.m.'

The three sentences are distinguishable in content alone, and illustrate that purposive and non-purposive locutions may have the common linguistic form which they exhibit. There is room, of

[1] A. K. Stout has made a very similar point in 'Free Will and Responsibility' (*P.A.S.*, 1936-37, p. 218).

course, for difference of opinion over precisely what the contents suggest as their correct interpretation.

My interpretation is that the first of them 'I am going to sneeze' most often occurs as a straightforward prediction of future fact expressing no purpose. Sneezing is most often an involuntary action, although sometimes it can be induced or repressed on purpose. Where it is involuntary, however, the sentence might conceivably be used to record an immediate experience, viz. the inclination to sneeze, rather than to make an inference about the future based on this inclination or nasal tickle. 'I am going to sleep' occupies an intermediate position within the triad in more than the spatial sense. It may occur as a simple prediction of what will occur quite apart from intention: or it may record the immediate feeling of drowsiness: or it may express the resolution to go to sleep. It does all three of these things according to context far more impartially, it seems to me, than its predecessor. Its successor 'I am going to catch the 9.30 a.m.' is in contrast to the other two far less subject to different interpretations. The contexts in which it could be interpreted as anything but an expression of purpose must be comparatively rare. One isn't often, for instance, shanghaied on to morning trains, and even if one were, it is doubtful that one would use the word 'catch' in quite these circumstances. Linguistic usage allows one to catch 'flu involuntarily but not trains.

It is clear enough now from this elucidation that in so far as any of the sentences within the triad qualify as expressions of purpose it is through the common form 'I am going to ... ' That is not enough, however, to invest them with the status of expressions of purpose. Over and above their formal aspect we have to consider the sort of action which they mention.

First, it seems that where the sort of action is such that one can infer it will occur without taking one's intention into consideration, then the predictive form expresses no purpose. (But I don't wish to suggest that the agent ever can list his intention among the data for prediction.) Sneezing and sleeping are commonly this sort of action, whereas catching a train is not. Furthermore, the peculiarity of catching a train which makes it intended is not, as Miss Anscombe might be interpreted as supposing,[1] a purely

[1] See *Intention* (Basil Blackwell, 1957), pp. 84ff.

linguistic peculiarity consisting in the way we describe the action. As I have already noticed, to describe catching a train as involuntary is linguistically odd: but this stems from the fact that the actual physical occurrences are generally not the sort to make it worth while to describe them in a more neutral manner. We could watch a film depicting a variety of actions with no written or spoken commentary, and still be able to determine which ones are more likely to be voluntary than the rest.

Second, where the action is such that one may feel a present tendency towards it without thereby becoming involved in doing it thereafter, or even feeling involved, then the predictive form which records this tendency expresses no purpose. Nasal tickles and the feeling of drowsiness have no necessary implications for the future. They need not be followed by sneezing or sleep, nor even lead to the expectation of the latter two. They are simply tendencies felt within the present.

Accordingly, whether a predictive form undeniably expresses purpose or not depends upon the sort of occurrence which it mentions. I don't wish to imply that some sorts can never figure in expressions of purpose, nor that others can never occur in predictions which don't express purpose. Some sorts, however, are more likely to do so than others, though at the same time there is no logical as distinct from causal limitation to the occurrences which can. It has also become evident just why some sorts of action are likely to be mentioned in expressions of purpose more frequently than others. In mentioning them it is clearer that the predictive form makes commitments about the future of a certain specific unique sort.

The predictive form is committed to the future in some way, first of all because the purpose which it expresses is definitely incompatible with any prediction of the same action which is committed to the future as an inference based on inductive grounds. No categorical predictive form mentioning the same action could on the same occasion have both the purposive and the inductive function, though it might be uncertain which function it had. How, then, can the purposive be incompatible with the inductive function, unless it too is committed to the future, though in some opposing manner? Secondly, it is committed to the future since its difference from a mere record of a felt present tendency consists in the latter having no necessary implications for the future. In some ways an expression of purpose seems to be intermediate between an inferred conclusion about the future and the record of an immediate felt tendency. It is like the former in being committed about the future. It is like the latter, and incompatible with the former, in being concerned with something immediate which is not the terminus of an inference. There seem strong grounds, then, for recognizing an expression of purpose as a statement about the future and as propositional if, in spite of its marked peculiarities, this is the only way of recognizing that these commitments are made by the meaning rather than the mere form of the expression.

It may seem possible, however, to express purpose by means of less committed and tendentious forms. To examine how far this is true I shall turn to contrasts which are more purely formal and so from now on I limit the form 'I am going to ... ' mainly to its purposive use. What the next two sets of contrasts have in common is that all the contrasted forms are predictive in some way and expressive of purpose.

(3) 'I am going to catch the 9.30 a.m.'
(4) 'I'll do my damnedest to catch the 9.30 a.m.'

Sentences (3) and (4), it will be observed, are both concerned with the same action, but each in a different way. This difference, however, doesn't prevent either from expressing a resolution to do a certain action: but the action mentioned by (4) is less determinate than the action mentioned by (3). Alternatively (4) mentions an action less specifically than (3). The action which (4) mentions isn't simply the catching of the 9.30 a.m. but a less determinate action which may or may not coincide with the catching of the 9.30 a.m.

But that is not the sole important difference between the two sentences. One has also to distinguish between the attitude they *express* and the attitude they *evince*. Every expression evinces but every evincing does not necessarily express what it evinces. For instance 'I'll do my damnedest, etc.', expresses a resolution as well as 'I am going to, etc.', but in certain contexts, while expressing resolution as effectively, though not as specifically as the latter, it may evince irresolution. Swearing often manifests uncertainty about oneself and one's aims. Expressing is, in the sense in which I propose to use the word 'expressing', not merely a manifestation of an attitude like tears of sorrow or a blush of embarrassment. In addition it is the *voluntary* manifestation for the purpose of communicating the fact that one has it. This last statement doesn't amount to a complete definition of 'expressing', but it may serve to check the sort of confusion between expressing and evincing shown, for instance, by the earlier exponents of the attitude theory in ethics.[1]

We now turn to a further group of contrasted expressions:

(3) 'I am going to catch the 9.30 a.m.'
(5) 'I am going to catch the 9.30 a.m., if I can'
(6) 'I'll try to catch the 9.30 a.m.'
(7) 'I'll do all within the bounds of reason to catch the 9.30 a.m.'

Like sentences (3) and (4), all members of this group mention in varying ways the same action. This should make clear that we must attend to the use of the different forms of expression *in the same context*. Of the group, it will be noticed (3) 'I am going to, etc.', is the sole sentence in which we have to specify a particular sort of content (catching the 9.30 a.m.) to make it quite clear that the sentence is expressive of resolution as well as predictive: unlike sneezing or sleeping, catching a train is unlikely to be anything but a voluntary action. The form of sentences (5)-(7), on the other hand, is such that the action which they mention specifically cannot be anything but voluntary if it comes off, whether it be sneezing, sleeping, or the catching of a train.

To prevent misunderstanding perhaps I should add one proviso. I have attributed a different significance to certain of these forms, when used in the same or in a similar context with reference to the same action or to similar actions, from the significance I attribute to others and especially to (3). But there may be circumstances in which expressions of one of these forms might do duty for others. It will be more convenient, however, if we confine our attention to circumstances in which together these expressions form an articulate system of meaning — where in other words one expression, and (3) in particular, would be used in preference to the others. Where, for instance, nobody doubts my

[1] Cf. A. J. Ayer, *Language, Truth and Logic*, 2nd ed., p. 107.

ability to catch the train, it is a matter of comparative indifference whether I express purpose by 'I am going to ... ', 'I am going to ... if I can', or 'I'll try to ... '; but where my ability is in doubt, it becomes necessary to discriminate.

Of all four expressions (3) 'I am going to, etc.', alone expresses specifically a resolution to act in a specific way. It expresses the speaker's resolution to catch the 9.30 a.m. The remaining expressions express some resolution, but because of their form they express no specific resolution specifically. They are unspecific expressions which (with the possible exception of (7) 'I'll do all within the bounds of reason, etc.') may *express*, albeit unspecifically, the specific resolution to perform a specific action, viz. the catching of the 9.30 a.m. On the other hand, they may equally well express as unspecifically a more moderate specific resolution to do a specific, but therein unspecified, action: the speaker may be uncertain whether the specific but unspecified action will eventuate in the specified action, viz. the catching of the 9.30 a.m. For instance, they may express unspecifically the resolution to rise in good time in the morning, or to buy one's ticket beforehand, or to make a reservation on the train, or all or more than one of these. At the same time they may anticipate some intervention which makes such precautions unavailing. Whatever the actual attitude these unspecific expressions do express, expression (3) remains in its form 'I am going to ... ' the specific expression of resolution: and this is true even supposing the action it actually specifies is not in fact the action the speaker has resolved to do.

As with sentence (4) 'I'll do my damnedest, etc.', it may, further, be possible to distinguish between what sentences (5) 'I am going to, etc., if I can' and (6) 'I'll try to, etc.', *express* and the attitude they *evince*. Emotionally they appear more neutral than a sentence of the form 'I'll do my damnedest ... ' like (4): they don't betray the excitability of the former. They have, however, because of their unspecific nature, a non-committal character which, according to the context, may or may not evince or betray attitudes incompatible with the resolution they express. The speaker may have chosen a comparatively non-committal form of expression because of a certain instability of resolution: or he may merely be uncertain about the causal connection between the specific but unspecified action he has resolved to do and the action which he specifies (e.g. between rising in good time, and catching the 9.30 a.m.): or again he may simply be unwilling to insist upon his actual certainty about the existence of this causal connection where he is willing that his listeners should remain in doubt. To take up the last point: unless an action is recognizably easy to perform, it may only become necessary or desirable to express specifically one's specific resolution, as in expression (3), where one must inspire confidence for the sake of success. It may be unsuitable, for instance, for a general delivering an eve-of-battle oration before his troops to say 'We shall try to sweep the enemy back' rather than 'We shall sweep the enemy back' or 'We are going to sweep the enemy back'.

The remaining expression (7) 'I'll do all within the bounds of reason, etc.', may neither express nor evince anything materially different from (5) 'I am going to, etc., if I can' or (6) 'I'll try to, etc.' Like them it does not refer to any specific action specifically: but it fails to do so in a rather different way. According to context the difference may or may not be significant. The phrase 'the bounds of reason' is highly unspecific in reference. This lack of specification may in certain contexts evince irresolution, but in others it may evince a negative resolution *not* to do certain kinds of action. However, in spite of these differences I propose in what follows to make (6) 'I'll try to, etc.', represent the three expressions in this group which are contrasted with (3) 'I am going to, etc.'

I have contrasted (3) as a specific expression of a specific resolution with other expressions which express specific resolutions unspecifically, in spite of their mentioning the same specific action (viz. catching the 9.30 a.m.). But I have no wish to deny that the less specific expressions may, in the particular circumstances of their utterance, be more warranted than (3). Indeed the statement 'I'll try to catch the 9.30 a.m.' may in certain circumstances appear so much more warranted than 'I am going to catch the 9.30 a.m.' as to throw grave doubt upon the authenticity of the latter as an expression of the specific resolution actually made by the speaker. In such circumstances (3) may be the evincing of *braggadocio* rather than the authentic expression of resolution. When the speaker sees that his chances of catching a train are remote if not altogether absent, 'I am going to catch the 9.30 a.m.' cannot be

F

regarded as the authentic expression of whatever resolution he may have made in the light of this knowledge. It is the tendentious nature of the 'I am going to ... ' form which may seem to make some more warranted substitute desirable.

But I have already emphatically declared that in this particular group of contrasted expressions where in common all express resolution, it is in the form of the expression that I am interested rather than their content or the action to which they specifically refer. An expression like 'I'll try to catch the 9.30 a.m.' may well be a more authentic expression of a *particular* resolution than 'I am going to catch the 9.30 a.m.' All I wish to insist is that whatever the agent's *specific* resolution, a sentence of the form 'I am going to ... ' gives more specific expression to this resolution than a sentence of some such form as 'I'll try to ... '

It may well be that where most specific actions are concerned a clear-headed agent may see that they are not the certain results of his efforts. Nevertheless, to refer to an action as, say, trying to catch the 9.30 a.m., is not to refer to that action in a specific manner, although it is to refer to the action the agent is *trying to do* specifically. If there is any such thing as a specific resolution at all, there must be some residual action which the agent in acting must feel confident that he can perform, and the resolution to perform such an action is specifically expressed by the form 'I am going to ... '

The consequences seem paradoxical of supposing that in the phrase 'trying to do A', where 'A' refers specifically to some action, the whole phrase refers specifically to a different sort of action which the agent can resolve to perform. If it refers specifically to some action other than A, it would seem that just in the same way as A may occur voluntarily or involuntarily so *trying* to do A may occur voluntarily or involuntarily, since like A it is the sort of thing we can resolve to do. But trying to do something is not the sort of thing we can do involuntarily unless we use 'involuntarily' in the rather borderline sense of 'acting under the threat of penalties'. Nor can trying be described without redundancy as voluntary. The reason for this is that 'trying to do A' refers unspecifically to some action which the agent does because he hopes or conjectures that it will result in A. Where we already refer implicitly or explicitly to an action as having been done in the hope of something, it is obviously redundant to go on to describe it as voluntary and inconsistent to describe it as involuntary.

At some stage, then, tendentiousness is inevitable. Although the specific expression of a given resolution may not be authentic either in part or in entirety, there always is present in the agent some resolution capable of authentic expression in the form 'I am going to ... ' — at least, in so far as he is capable of voluntary actions at all. Of course, at no moment is it ever impossible for him, provided he has time, to reflect that what he resolves to do he may not do successfully. This doubt, however, need be no more than a purely theoretical doubt which doesn't modify the resolution in any way. When the resolution is of the residual kind (i.e. where the action resolved upon cannot be subdivided into a subsequent part about the occurrence of which the agent is relatively uncertain and an antecedent part about the occurrence of which he is relatively certain), then the doubt or reflection must be purely theoretical.

A doubt of this purely theoretical kind must be carefully distinguished from other kinds of doubt which would lead one to express resolution by 'I'll try to catch the 9.30 a.m.' rather than by 'I am going to catch the 9.30 a.m.' If the doubt were of the purely theoretical kind in this instance, there could be no other resolution than the resolution to catch the 9.30 a.m., for, whichever of the two expressions we employ to express resolution, it is the resolution to catch the 9.30 a.m. which is thereby expressed. The agent's reasons for refusing definitely to assert that his specific project is practicable would not be peculiar just to that particular situation in which he has to act. He is not in doubt, for instance, because he realizes that his other commitments might prevent him from setting out in time to catch the 9.30 a.m. That would not be a doubt about all specific projects, but simply doubt about the practicability of one particular project or a definite number of particular projects as against certain other more moderate projects. Just because the agent doubts his ability to catch the 9.30 a.m. he might not doubt his ability to get up in the morning in good time for catching the 9.30 a.m.

Before allowing ourselves to accept finally the conclusion that the tendentious 'I am going to ... ' is the sole form for giving expression specifically to specific resolutions we should, however, take notice of one other group of contrasted expressions, viz.:

(3) 'I am going to catch the 9.30 a.m.'
(8.1) 'I intend to catch the 9.30 a.m.'
(8.2) 'I am resolved to catch the 9.30 a.m.'
(8.3) 'I purpose to catch the 9.30 a.m.'
(8.4) 'I have decided to catch the 9.30 a.m.'

Here I have labelled the new sentences by decimal numbers to play down whatever difference in shade of meaning each may owe to its linguistic difference from the rest. Sentence (8.1) can be taken as typifying the rest, and accordingly I shall for convenience refer to it as '(8)'. For my present purpose the contrast between these sentences and (3) 'I am going to, etc.', is of sole importance.

The contrast presented here differs, it will be observed, from the preceding. It cannot be said that (8) 'I intend to, etc.', expresses, as does 'I'll try to, etc.', a specific resolution unspecifically. It seems to mention the resolution as specifically as it could be mentioned. But just because it mentions the specific resolution neither can it be said to express it specifically. It does not express it at all — except implicitly. I don't wish to become embroiled here in a general discussion of what has been called the parenthetical uses of verbs as in 'I believe that ... ', 'I wish that ... ', and finally 'I intend to ... ' All that one need bear in mind for our present purpose is the contrast between this set of introductory phrases and sentences such as 'That is the case', 'Would that that were the case', and finally 'I am going to etc.' The latter give expression to the attitudes which the introductory phrases respectively mention.

Sometimes, indeed, it may seem that by using the introductory phrases we diminish in some way the attitudes which they mention and the quoted sentences respectively express. Instead, then, of expressing the attitude implicitly by mentioning it, it may seem that we express something rather more pusillanimous. 'I believe that is the case' may seem to have the same force as 'Probably that is the case'. This impression, however, rests on a confusion between what these verbs may evince and what they make explicit. Their function, in so far as they have a common one, is mainly to enable the speaker explicitly to speak for himself where he wishes to indicate that his audience may not underwrite or corroborate his attitude. This explicit function expresses implicitly the same attitude as the quoted sentences, though at the same time it may evince pusillanimity — a going over to the other side as it were.

There may, however, seem to be special reasons for questioning this interpretation in its application to the attitude of intention. Intentions are revocable, and they are also fallible in the sense that one may intend to do what in fact is impossible to perform. In consequence of these universally recognized facts it may seem that (3) 'I am going to, etc.', is unnecessarily bold or too committed as an expression of purpose. To be resolute one has to be bold in action, but not, it may seem, about facts. Why shouldn't one instead use something more non-committal such as 'I intend to …' as an explicit expression of purpose? A closer look at the reasons for this proposal shows, however, that they have been misunderstood.

Intentions are revocable, it is true. One can make up one's mind to do something, and then change one's mind and decide to do something else. To intend to do an action is even consistent with not trying or beginning to do it rather than some alternative, provided the intention is formed and revoked before it can become operative in that respect, even though it must be operative in some respect. But although an agent may revoke his intentions, any intention of his must implicitly at least exclude the intention at a later date to revoke it. It is absurd to say 'I intend to go away tomorrow, but when I rise in the morning I will cancel my intention'. The form 'I intend to …', in other words, implicitly commits one to what the form 'I am going to …' expressly commits one to. The latter alone, however, makes the inconsistency absolutely explicit since 'I am not going to …' is the explicit expression for revoking an intention. The two explicit expressions explicitly contradict each other.

It is also true that we may intend to do what is in fact incapable of performance. But here once again a similar principle limits what the agent may believe when intending. One cannot intend to do anything unless at the time one believes that it lies within one's power to do it. It is equally absurd to say 'I intend to go away tomorrow, but in fact will be unable to do so'. Once again the implicit inconsistency is made explicit when we recognize that 'I am going to ... ' is the form which gives direct explicit expression to purpose. 'I am unable to ... ' confutes 'I am going to ... ' in an explicit manner which we shall examine more closely in the next chapter. In intending, then, the commitments of the predictive form 'I am going to ... ' are unavoidable.

In this investigation of the direct and most explicit form which expresses purpose it has also become plainer just why the specific categorical predictive form and none other qualifies for this function. The reasons are logical rather than conventional. It doesn't qualify as an expression of purpose in the way in which 'Alas!', for instance, qualifies as an expression of sorrow. Practically any other ejaculation could have come to fulfil the function of the latter as effectively. The implications of all the terminology connected with purpose make it clear, on the other hand, that it is through its direct specific and categorical mention of the future that the predictive form 'I am going to ... ' expresses purpose. Without this mention purpose could not be expressed so explicitly. In the following chapter I shall consider precisely how to interpret this. Can we accept that expressions of purpose are genuine predictions?

CHAPTER VII

THE SINGULARITY OF THE FUTURE

IF expressions of purpose are predictions at all we must recognize that they are predictions of a very curious kind indeed. To see this we need only extend our attention to a fourth set of contrasts. In the course of investigating these I hope to show

(a) that neither the mental-event nor the Rylean analysis of intention is severally or in conjunction logically adequate; for neither do justice to the standpoint of the agent;

(b) that in fact Libertarianism alone can meet the requirements of the logic of expressions of purpose.

I

The set of contrasts consists of three main groups of sentences already considered in the previous chapter all of which incorporate the use of the first person singular as compared against similar sentences which incorporate the third person singular instead.

(i)	I am going	} to sneeze
(ii)	He is going	
(3)	I am going	} to catch the 9.30 a.m.
(iii)	He is going	
(8)	I intend	} to catch the 9.30 a.m.
(viii)	He intends	

In place of the sentence marked by Roman numerals one could substitute certain other sentences without altering the point of the contrast. The personal pronoun which is the subject can be in the second person singular ('thou' or 'you'), in the second person plural ('you'), in the third person singular ('he' or 'she'), and in the third person plural ('they'). Alternatively these sentences can have first person singular subjects ('I') provided the tense of the main verb is changed from the present or future indicative to the past indicative. As a matter of convenience, however, we can take the form they actually do assume above as representative of all these variants.

The point of the contrast is that even where we take (3) 'I am going to catch the 9.30 a.m.' and (iii) 'He is going to catch the 9.30 a.m.' as uttered by different persons but about the same action of the same agent, we nevertheless cannot take them as logically equivalent to each other. There are really no commonly accepted technical terms in logic to mark the precise difference. We might say as a preliminary to further explanation that they have a common meaning content but that their logical status is different. The difference isn't simply that they express the belief attitudes of different people. This is equally true within the other two groups (1) (i) and (8) (viii). In the instance of (3) (iii), on the contrary, this difference in the owner of the belief attitude seems to mark some much more distinctive difference between (3) and (iii). It makes (3) 'I am going to, etc.', an expression of purpose and (iii) 'He is going to, etc.', merely an expression of predictive belief about an intentional action.

It may prove instructive here to compare (3) 'I am going to, etc.', with Professor Austin's performatives.[1] There is an important logical difference between 'I bet' and 'He bets', 'I promise' and 'He promises', 'I give' and 'He gives', etc., where in each pair the 'I' and the 'He' indicate the same person on the same occasion. This difference is quite different from that between, say, 'I am writing ... ' and 'He is writing ... ' I bet, promise, and give, etc., by saying 'I bet', 'I promise', and 'I give' in the appropriate circumstances, but I don't write by saying 'I am writing ... ' According to Austin what he calls 'performative expressions' are primarily performances. These performances presuppose the existence of some ritual or convention whereby one does certain things by making in appropriate circumstances these sounds or affixing one's signature to these marks. The function of such expressions is not to refer or describe. On the other hand, the expressions in the third person form describe respectively the performance completed by uttering the sentence in the first person form with which they have been paired above.

Obviously there is a radical logical disparity between these paired expressions which suggests that a parallel disparity between

---

[1] To the best of my knowledge Austin's work on performatives remains unpublished except in peripheral form as in 'Other Minds' (*Logic and Language*: Second Series, ed. by A. G. N. Flew).

(3) 'I am going, etc.', and (iii) 'He is going, etc.', may stem from the respective use of first and third person singular pronouns. At the same time the difference between Austin's performatives, on the one hand, and expressions of purpose, on the other, is of equal significance. Expressions of purpose are not the exercise of some ritual or convention, except in the way that any linguistic expression is such. Their logical peculiarity actually does not pertain primarily to their linguistic form at all. I can intend to catch a train without announcing what I am about to do, and the logical peculiarities of expressions of intention are the peculiarities of the intention or curious sort of belief which is expressed. I am catching a train in *believing* rather than in *predicting* that I will.

In what follows I shall for the sake of convenience refer to the sort of attitude expressed by (3) 'I am going to, etc.', as the standpoint of the agent. In contrast what (iii) 'He is going to, etc.', expresses is the standpoint of the other agent towards the first, or, in more convenient terms, the alien standpoint.[1] Expressed more precisely the distinction which I wish to examine is between the standpoint of the agent at the moment of action towards his projected action, on the one hand, and the standpoint of any other agent towards the first agent and his action, or the standpoint of the same agent towards his own past or non-projected actions, on the other hand. The distinction is such that any standpoint towards any agent, whatever it may be, must belong to one or other kind. There is no fence between them on which one can sit, though it is possible while having one standpoint to be in imaginative possession of the other. Furthermore, everybody must hold both standpoints, but not towards the same person or action.

My confining the agent's standpoint to the moment of action may perhaps seem a bit restrictive. Can one not decide, intend, or project some time before the consonant action is called for? It seems to me that though in a sense one can, yet a decision or intention, to qualify as such, must always be in some sense opera-

---

[1] This distinction is modelled upon the contrast between the self as agent and the self as subject drawn (cf. *The Self as Agent*, chap. IV) by Professor John Macmurray, to whose teaching my debt is incalculable. My version is designed to forestall any effort to divorce the practical from the theoretical outlook, and to suggest instead that the difference is between ways in which the practical outlook is directed. It has affinities as well to Sartre's distinction between *l'être pour soi* and *l'être pour l'autrui* (cf. *L'être et le néant*, pp. 310ff).

tive, though not necessarily with success. My decision to holiday in a particular country next year is certainly made some time previous to the specified action but it qualifies as decision only because I put myself in a state of readiness towards that end. It involves trying to begin to wend one's way down the intervening chain of possibilities in such a way as not to exclude the possibility of holidaying in the selected place when the time comes round.

We can now introduce in convenient form the more positive conclusion of this chapter which I shall support in later sections. I shall argue that from the alien standpoint some sort of distinction between the agent's intending to do something and his actually being about or going to do something is unavoidable. From the alien standpoint the agent's intending to do something is one of the things which the alien has to take into account in predicting what the agent actually is about to or going to do. The fact that the agent is about to do something consists, it may seem legitimate to suppose, in some sort of connective relation between the action which the agent is about to do and the agent's standpoint or decision that he is about to do it. From the agent's standpoint, on the other hand, no distinction between his intending to do something and the fact that he is going to or about to do it can properly be made. Where from the alien standpoint a distinction has to be made between a subjective factor consisting in the agent's intention and an objective fact consisting in the agent's being about to do something which the subjective factor conditions in some way, from the agent's standpoint on the other hand no such distinction between a subjective factor of the same sort and an objective fact which it conditions exists at all. From the agent's standpoint these two things disappear as it were into each other. This, then, is what the different logical status of (3) 'I am going to, etc.', and (iii) 'He is going to, etc.', amounts to.

It follows that the two standpoints, alien's and agent's, constitute two different conceptual frameworks, though as we shall see in the next chapter the former is subordinate to the latter since the alien is an agent as well. Considerable caution has to be exercised in keeping them conceptually distinct. Bradley's pronouncement,[1] for instance, that Libertarianism makes it impossible for a man to know what in the world he will be doing next, seems

[1] See Chapter I.

to show confusion between them. From the alien standpoint alone the fact that the agent is about to do something can plausibly be considered to require a complete antecedent condition if its aboutness is to exist, is to be explicable, or is to be known. From the agent's standpoint the fact that he is about to do something can have no such complete antecedent condition. For him his intention and his aboutness disappear into each other in the sort of situation where for others the antecedent conditions of the action he is about to do would be incomplete without his intention. His aboutness from his standpoint must be explicable in an entirely different way which I investigate in Chapter IX.

2

What follows is a sort of *reductio ad absurdum* designed to confirm the conclusion I have just formulated. It consists of an attempt to force the standpoint of the agent into the conceptual framework which could only be appropriate to the alien standpoint with a consistency and rigour normally shirked by those who think that this sort of thing is in principle possible. The assumption that it is possible is a very natural one since in using language for the purpose of communication we are bound so far as possible to sink as it were our personal differences and to try to understand the propositional content of our utterances as possessing an impersonal logical status. Because of this tendency a *reductio ad absurdum* which carries it beyond its legitimate sphere is of particular therapeutic value.

Our point of departure is the prediction (iii) 'He is going to, etc.' What precisely are we assuming when we make this prediction as a prediction of an intentional action? It is perfectly innocuous to say for a start that anyone who makes a prediction of this sort implies in some sense of the word 'imply' that two main conditions are satisfied, viz. that the action will be in accordance with the agent's intention and that it comes about in some way through the agent's intention. Harmless though it is, however, this solution is not quite good enough: it even fails to take account of what we already know about intention, viz. that it finds expression in such predictions as (3) 'I am going to, etc.' Accordingly it may seem both natural and necessary to expand these two conditions into three as follows:

(*a*) the agent must believe that his prediction is true, i.e. it must be authentic;

(*b*) the fulfilment of (*a*) must be a necessary condition of the truth of the prediction;

(*c*) he must believe (*b*).

The first and last of these conditions are conditions of the appropriate action being in accordance with the agent's intention. The second condition, on the other hand, is the condition of the action taking place through the agent's intention.

This analysis of the conditions of intentional action derives a certain amount of intuitive support from examples. In support of the first condition let us take an action, which the agent says will happen but at no stage believes will happen, and which actually does happen. He may for instance in downing a pint of beer say 'I am going to get drunk', not believe it, and forthwith become tight. In this case we couldn't say his intoxication was intentional or even voluntary. If, on the other hand, the agent really does believe what he says, we still cannot in all cases suppose his action to be intentional. He may say 'I am going to be sick', believe it, and forthwith vomit: but yet the action is not intentional.

Accordingly we seem directed towards the second condition that where the agent believes his action will come about, his believing it will come about must be a necessary condition of the action coming about, if the action in coming about is intentional rather than a more or less happy fluke. This additional condition, however, is still insufficient to make the occurrence of the action intentional. It might be the case, for instance, that unless the agent had thought he was about to become sick and had felt additionally nauseated at the prospect he wouldn't have become sick at all. Or more obviously still, people often are failures because they think they are failures, and strictly failure cannot be intentional. Or again, a patient may recover from what the doctors believed to be a fatal illness simply because he believed the intended lie by which they allayed his anxiety in predicting his recovery. His recovery is not an intentional one even though it was in accordance with his most earnest wish.

Before we can class an action which occurs as occurring intentionally it seems, then, we have to satisfy ourselves that the third condition has been fulfilled consisting in the agent's believing that his believing in the occurrence of his action is a necessary condition of the action coming about. People, for instance, who have the faculty of curing themselves by faith, but not merely through the agency of doctors' lies, could be said to have made an intentional recovery. Their action would be directly connected with decision in the same way as when I wag my little finger intentionally this is directly connected in some way with my decision to do so.

One may wonder whether any further conditions besides these three may seem required when we say of an action which actually comes about that it comes about intentionally. Could there be cases where the agent believes the action will come about, and believes correctly that his believing this or its negative is a necessary condition of the action coming about as believed, while yet even when the action does come about as believed it does not do so as an intentional action? There does in fact seem to be room for another condition which can, however, be treated as an elucidation of (*a*) and (*c*).

Take once again the example of faith cure. Either my unshakeable belief in my recovery in certain specific circumstances is rational or irrational. In other words, either it has been formed in consideration of the causal potentialities of the situation, or it hasn't. This consideration may have been more or less complex as we shall see in Chapter VIII. The consideration in the light of which I do things directly under my control such as wag my finger can best be described negatively. The fact, for instance, that my hand is not in a plaster cast is one of them. The decision to play the piano, in contrast, is made in consideration of more positive factors such as the presence of a piano. Now if my belief that I am going to do something has no pretensions to rationality of these kinds, it is quite possible to see how I could correctly hold a second belief that this belief is a necessary condition of what I am going to do, or the state I am about to be in, without that action or state being in any way intentional.

Prior to making a proposal of marriage I may boost my self-confidence by taking a swig from my hip-flask, or prior to sitting an exam I may dose myself with benzedrine for the same purpose, or yet again in order to recover from an illness I may put myself in the charge of someone with the particular form of hypnotic personality peculiar to those who effect faith-cures. At the time, however, I conceivably might judge from the small inner core of the mind into which my self-consciousness has retreated that the confidence in my ability to carry the action out according to plan is a necessary condition without which I would fail. This may not of course be the precise manner in which such expedients work. Alcohol or benzedrine, for instance, may just steady one's nerves or help concentration without in any way inducing non-rational confidence in one's abilities: but for the sake of the argument I am supposing that they have this effect as well. In such circumstances, then, one might well hesitate to say that the success of my proposal of marriage, candidature as an examinee, or recovery from sickness comes about as fully through my intention as if I hadn't relied upon these expedients. It would depend, I think, upon just how much of my total action one takes into consideration. During the actual process of proposing, writing, or concentrating on my recovery it could be said that I am little better than an automaton. But in so far as I know how to control myself as an automaton for certain purposes by putting myself under various sorts of influence, full responsibility for the action belongs to me.

With the proviso, then, that the agent's belief that his action will come about is a rational one we seem to have formulated all the conditions under which an action which actually does come about is fully intentional. It will be observed, however, that these conditions have a striking recursive aspect. Their propositional content exhibits internal relations which may lead one to suspect that the triple conditioning develops from some pretty radical logical flaw in our initial move. This flaw will become more manifest as we probe further.

We must to begin with examine more carefully the precise manner of implication in which a statement that an action is intentional can be said to imply that these conditions have been fulfilled. There are in all three kinds of implication between which we must be careful to distinguish.

The first kind is the sort which is sometimes called logical implication. This name is misleading because it covers causal implication as well as other kinds. Their true distinguishing feature consists of the validity of the law of contraposition. If p implies q in this way then not-q implies not-p. The statement that if anything is a rose then it is a flower implies by contraposition that if anything is not a flower then it is not a rose. Consequently I shall call the sort of implication exhibited here by 'if ... then' 'contrapositable implication'. As quite distinct from this we must recognize the sort of implication which according to Strawson holds between 'The present King of France is bald' and 'There is a King of France'. According to Strawson,[1] though the former proposition implies the latter, the latter is a condition of the application of the former rather than of its truth. In other words, the latter is a condition both of the truth and the falsity of the former. If the latter is false then the former is neither true nor false. Hence implication through contrasposition does not take place here because, although p implies q, not-q implies the negative conjunction neither p nor not-p instead of simply not-p. One could call this 'contextual implication' were it not that Nowell-Smith has used this label more widely.[2] Instead I shall call it 'applicational implication'. Thirdly, we must recognize as distinct the sort of relation which holds between 'There are tigers in Bengal' and 'I believe there are tigers in Bengal' where the former is what expresses the latter. From the fact that 'There are tigers in Bengal' implies 'I believe there are tigers in Bengal', when uttered on the same occasion by the same speaker, one cannot infer that 'It is not the case that I believe there are tigers in Bengal' implies 'There are not tigers in Bengal'. In this case, though p implies q, not-q merely implies that it is out of place for the speaker to affirm p, because he would thereby express a contradictory belief: but nothing can be inferred about the truth or falsity or even the application of p. This is one sort of implication which Nowell-Smith calls 'contextual' but I shall call it 'expressive'.

Now let us consider in which of these three ways the various conditions of intentional action can be said to be implied. We can agree at the outset that most statements, with the possible exception of those in stories, imply expressively a statement of the form 'I believe ... ' There would be nothing exceptional then about expressions of purpose if this turned out to be the sole manner in

---

[1] 'On Referring', *Essays in Conceptual Analysis*, ed. A. G. N. Flew.
[2] *Ethics* (Pelican), pp. 80-7.

which they seem to imply that the agent believes in them. But as we shall see this is not the sole way.

The first condition that the agent believes that the action will come about, and the third condition that he also believes that his believing this is a necessary condition of its being true, are as we have seen conditions of the action taking place *in accordance with* the agent's intention. Thus they can conveniently be taken in conjunction. Now these conditions are implied equally where (iii) 'He is going to, etc.', is advanced as a prediction of an intentional action, and where it is withdrawn by 'He will fail to, etc.' Failing to do what has been intended requires their fulfilment just as much as succeeding to do it. Hence we have here an instance of applicational implication where the law of contraposition does not hold. It obviously is not an instance of expressive implication since no statement can expressively imply the belief of somebody other than the speaker.

The same sort of conclusion holds for the second condition that the agent's believing his action will come about is a necessary condition of its coming about. This is a condition of the action coming about *through* the agent's intention. In other words, where this condition is the only one to be unfulfilled we say in the event of the action coming about that it came about coincidentally. The agent may have assessed the situation incorrectly. He may, for instance, set about shutting a door which can only shut automatically or curing by faith a disease which faith doesn't in the least affect. Here we would not attribute the shut door, or health restored, to his intention. In what way, then, is this condition implied?

It is not necessarily implicit, to begin with, in the agent's failing to do the action he attempts. If it were, it would be implicit in the same way as the other two conditions. But if an agent tries to shut an automatically closing door and the automatic mechanism jams, one could say that he fails to shut the door without supposing that his belief that the door was going to shut is a necessary condition of the door's shutting. Only where the door is not automatic and jams when the agent sets about shutting it, would one be prepared to say that his belief that the action would come about is as much a condition of failure as of the door being successfully shut. These examples illustrate that some additional factor apart from the presence of the second condition is involved in those instances where the second condition is a condition both of success and failure. We must first find what it is if we wish to understand better the way in which the second condition operates.

We have now to attend to an entirely different sort of condition for the coming about of an intentional action. It consists of the circumstances of the action. The fact that the 9.30 a.m. is running as scheduled is, for example, a condition of the agent's catching it. It belongs to the circumstances he assumes when he makes his decision. It is not, however, a straightforward condition of the contrapositable kind of (iii) 'He is going to, etc.', since it is equally a condition of 'He is not going to, etc.', where the latter predicts a negatively intentional action. If the speaker thought that unknown to the agent a condition of this sort was lacking he might say 'He'll try to, etc.', or 'He'll not try to etc.', instead. In short a condition of this sort is a condition of ability. If it does not hold, the agent is unable to perform the action, and therefore it is equally pointless to consider whether through intention (the second condition) he will or will not do it.

We can now understand more clearly the second condition, that the agent's belief that the action will come about is a necessary condition of its coming about. If this condition does not hold one could not say either that the agent is able to perform the action or that he is unable to perform the action. Where, for instance, he sets about shutting a door which can only shut automatically and actually is at the moment shutting, this second condition does not hold. Here it seems equally misleading to say that he can shut the door and to say that he cannot shut the door. Where, on the other hand, he sets about shutting a less sophisticated sort of door, this condition does hold, and it does seem relevant once again to say that he can or cannot shut the door, depending upon whether it fits its frame properly, etc. Now since this second condition is a condition both of ability and inability, and since in the preceding paragraph we saw that conditions of ability are implied applicationally by (iii) 'He is going to, etc.', it follows *a fortiori* that the second condition is implied applicationally by (iii) as well.

This completes, then, our review of the mode of implication

G

peculiar to the three conditions of the intentionality of an action which occurs.

3

Now comes the reckoning. The assumption upon which most of the preceding reasoning has been based is that predictive expressions of the form 'I am going to ... ' and 'He is going to ... ' are always confirmable in the same sort of way. More specifically, we have been assuming that when the former expresses purpose and the latter refers to the same person and action as the former mentions, then, whatever the other differences between them, they are confirmable in the same sort of way.

Let us inspect once again the conditions in terms of which this confirmation is supposed to be possible. They are:

(a) the agent must believe that his prediction is true, i.e. it must be authentic;

(b) the fulfilment of (a) must be a necessary condition of the truth of the prediction;

(c) he must believe (b).

We also recognized the further proviso, or elucidation of (a) and (c), that the agent's belief that his action will come about is a rational one. But the implications of this are viciously regressive for reasons already anticipated in the previous chapter. Condition (c) requires that if the agent proceeds rationally then he can satisfy (a) only if he believes (b), but (b) requires him not to believe that the prediction is true unless (a) is satisfied; i.e. he isn't entitled to believe that the prediction is true unless and until he believes that he believes that the prediction is true. The conditions as set out are in other words circular and recursive.

Now at first sight it may seem that the logical scandal pertains solely to the agent whose confirmation procedure has been constrained to revolve in an eternal circle. This would be bad enough. A protracted effort to bring the agent's standpoint within the province of inductively confirmable predictions has demonstrated that inductive standards can only be brought to bear upon his predictive activities in an illogical manner. We haven't merely represented the agent as a man who doesn't know what in the world he is going to do next, as Bradley taunts the Libertarian with doing. That would merely represent the agent as non-rational. More scandalously, by pressing what Bradley would have regarded as rational standards upon the agent, we have made his attitude radically irrational.

In a different way, however, the alien standpoint is in no better case. The alien can take conditions (a), (b), and (c) as a basis for his prediction 'He is going to ... ' But it now turns out that these conditions are really insufficient in number so long as he fails to distinguish the confirmation procedures of his own predictive belief from those of the agent. Handicapped in this way, he must believe that the agent as well, in so far as he is rationally guided, must take conditions (a), (b), and (c) as satisfied before making his prediction. We must remember, too, that the proviso that the agent is rationally guided was one which we read into the other conditions. But this immediately adds a further condition (d) to the conditions with which the agent must reckon in making his prediction. Condition (d) can be formulated with greater or lesser economy in view of the internal relations holding between the other three, but we need not go into that matter now. It should now be clear that the same considerations which lead to the supplementation of (a), (b), and (c) by (d) must require the supplementation of (a), (b), (c), and (d) by a fifth condition (e). These same considerations will in fact reapply an infinite number of times and lead to an infinite regress, so that the conditions for the prediction can never be complete.

The solution to this tangle is quite simple. Confirmation procedures for 'He is going to ... ' need involve no regress once we realize that 'I am going to ... ' enjoys a logical status which is quite unique. Only two conditions apart from more objective ones are in fact required by the procedure, viz.:

(a^1) 'I am going to ... ' expresses the agent's purpose authentically;
(b^1) the fulfilment of (a^1) is a necessary condition of the action purposed.

This, too, of course, is just another way of saying that the action must be in accordance with the agent's intention and done through the agent's intention.

By classifying the expression of purpose as a belief or as propositional we expose ourselves to the danger of supposing that
its difference from 'He is going to ... ' is no greater than the difference between any other pair of expressions in the first and third
persons singular respectively which make mention of the same
person and action. The danger becomes particularly acute when
we try to put the agent's expression of purpose into indirect
speech. We would then find it natural to say that the agent
believes that he is going to, etc., where the subordinate noun
clause is in the third person predictive form. Ordinary usage, of
course, has its defences against the possibility of this confusion,
since frequently we don't put the agent's expression of purpose
into indirect speech. When referring to it we quite frequently say
instead simply that the agent intends to do such-and-such.

In any case, whatever is the root of the confusion, it is only
when we try to vulgarize or depersonalize the content of the
expression in this way that it becomes necessary to express the
condition that the action is in accordance with the agent's intention as composite consisting of conditions (a) and (c). We stipulate (c) as a condition in an unavailing effort to restore (a) to its
proper singularity, rather as millers 'reinforce' nowadays the
national loaf with some of the properties extracted from the flour
by modern methods of milling. By stipulating that the agent
believes that his believing is a necessary condition of his prediction's truth, or the predicted action's performance, we try to impose upon the agent an account of the singularity of his expression
which is appropriate to the alien alone, viz. condition (b). Since
this brings his account into alignment with the alien's, we have,
accordingly, once again to impose the further condition (d) that
the agent must believe that (c) as well as (a) is a necessary condition of the action's performance, and so on *ad infinitum*.

Once we detect the cause of the infinite regress, the positive
conclusion which I announced at the beginning of the chapter can
be seen to follow. The agent cannot regard his intending as something distinguishable from his being about to do the action which
he intends to do. The distinction becomes conceivable from the
alien standpoint alone. Now before we had detected the precise
cause of the recursiveness in the conditions of an intentional action
being performed, the only conclusion which we could deduce

from the recursiveness was that it is logically impossible to predict the performance of the action on inductive grounds. This conclusion, however, might seem to have had no ontological implications, and in particular to be still consistent with a deterministic account of the causal conditions of the action. Once the cause of the regress has been located, on the other hand, the indeterministic implications are apparent. Where the action which comes about intentionally takes place, its conditions are incomplete apart from the fact that it comes about through the agent's intention. Consequently from the standpoint from which the distinction between the agent's being about to do the action and his intention to do it disappears, his being about to do it must be incompletely conditioned without further qualification. This has similar implications for the alien standpoint as well, which we shall consider in the next section.

One doubt at least about this ontological conclusion may, however, remain. It may seem too firmly wedded to my assumption that expressions of purpose are propositional. I shall examine this assumption more carefully in the next section. My previous chapter, however, has already shown that whether they are propositional or not they are committed to the future in more than verbal form, and the arguments by which this was established are enough to establish my conclusions in this section without further assumption. We saw that an authentic expression of purpose definitely precludes the agent from believing he is unable to perform the action, or that he will change his mind. It in fact implies in some sense that the action will be performed whether it says this or not. Consequently it cannot allow any external relation between the agent's intention and his being about to perform the action. Otherwise it would have to allow intention to be a condition of the action which could be fulfilled independently of the objective necessary conditions of the action. It would be logically impeccable to say 'I intend it, but the other conditions of its occurrence are not fulfilled'. Accordingly, given the findings of my previous chapter the indeterministic implications of the agent's expression of purpose stand, whether my assumption about its propositional status is correct or not.

4

In coming to the preceding conclusions two points have been left unresolved. The first consists of the question which I may seem this moment to have dismissed as no longer crucial, viz. 'Are expressions of purpose propositional?' The second is the question whether one is entitled to assume, as in the preliminary stages of my argument I seemed content to do, that from the alien as distinct from the agent's point of view the fact that something is about to happen consists in the present existence of complete conditions of its coming about.

While the first question remains unresolved my account of the future commitments of purpose must seem less then perspicuous, and my whole distinction between standpoints in consequence tainted with some doubt. My version of practical knowledge as the agent's standpoint can hardly stand if the latter turns out to be inexpressible as such in propositional form. My previous chapter, of course, disposes directly of some of the reasons offered in support of contrary findings — those, for instance, which represent resolution simply as undertaking to *try* to do something.[1] If there is any such thing as specific resolution, then the straightforward prediction of the specific action considered is its most accurate expression. And the fact that this expression does not raise the question whether the intended action will be successful or fail is not due to the fact that the predictive form is not predictive in content, as Hampshire suggests, but due simply to there being no distinction from the agent's standpoint between intending and being about to act. Other causes for doubt may, however, remain.

The analogy which I have used in the course of my argument between expressions of purpose and Austin's performatives, may, for instance, suggest that I have succumbed to the fallacy which he so vigorously castigated, viz. that of supposing all indicative sentences to be 'statemental', 'constative', or propositional. In the same way as it seems beside the point to ask whether 'I promise', 'I bet', etc., are true or false on typical occasions of their utterance, so, one might argue, to describe an expression of

---

[1] See Stuart Hampshire, *Thought and Action*, pp. 112-13.

purpose as true or false is equally inappropriate. This point does have a superficial plausibility.

There are a considerable number of ways in which an expression of purpose may be confuted. This can easily leave the impression that to challenge its truth is to miss its point. 'I am going to, etc.', may be followed by a change of mind on the part of the agent, which he expresses by 'I am not going to do so after all'. This is to express a negative intention. Again, its authenticity or sincerity may be questioned by another agent. The latter may deny that the agent is going to act as announced on the grounds that the agent doesn't really intend to act in this way. This is to treat it more like the giving of an undertaking. Or again, the other agent may say something like 'Yes, you most certainly are, for I am going to make you, whether you like it or not'. In this instance he is expressing an intention of his own in response to the agent's expression. Yet again, the other agent may believe that the agent intends to do what he announces, but wish to deny that it will come about through his intention, or alternatively that it will come about through an intention based upon an informed appraisal of the circumstances. He may say 'Yes, as a matter of fact you will. You can't very well help doing otherwise', or 'Yes, you will, though not quite in the way you think'. Finally, the other agent may confute the agent's expression of purpose simply by saying 'You can't, and therefore you won't'.

Of all the methods of confutation, and those listed here are by no means exhaustive, the last alone is of the most typically factual kind. It is on similar considerations that one refutes ordinary predictions of the gambling or inductive kinds. Nobody, say, will ever run a mile in under two minutes in standard conditions, because this is physically impossible, and for this reason we say it is false that some day the mile will be run in under two minutes. Now since this sort of appraisal of truth or falsity is only one of the different sorts of appraisal which as we have seen seem at least just as relevant to expressions of purpose, can we justifiably use it as a basis for classing expressions of purpose as propositional? One might regard such expressions as more analogous to the class of performatives in which we give estimates or pass verdicts. As Austin pointed out, when one uses 'I estimate that it took at least twenty years to build this cathedral' to give an estimate, one is not saying anything true or false, but is saying something which is correct or incorrect depending on its factual basis.

Is there any justification then for regarding expressions of purpose as propositional? I must admit that one does, in most circumstances that one can imagine, feel rather unhappy about describing any expression of purpose as true or false without further qualification. Accordingly if we define a proposition as anything which is either true or false perhaps one should feel equally unhappy about describing expressions of purpose as propositional. There are, however, good negative and positive reasons for overcoming this uneasiness and for attributing it to the profound difference between expressions of purpose and other types of proposition which I hope to clarify.

To begin with the negative reasons: expressions of purpose are not performatives. No doubt they are speech acts, for any use of language is a speech act of some sort. But they are expressive acts, whereas performatives are not. The function of expression implies the existence of some activity or state which need not take overt verbal form and which the expression expresses. This activity or state is distinct then from the overt verbal form. In enunciating performatives such as 'I promise that, etc.', or 'I estimate that this costs, etc.', on the other hand, the activity of promising or giving an estimate just is the saying of these things in the appropriate context. At the same time, of course, they give expression to intentions and beliefs in an indirect way: but what they give expression to isn't the promising or the estimating, for that is just what they are. Also the intentions and beliefs to which they give expression could be expressed by speech acts which are not promises or estimates but just expressions. A locution is performative only in so far as it is other than or more than an expression. The only true parallel I can find between expressions of purpose and performatives presupposes indeed that the two are quite distinct. If I have been correct in supposing that just as one bets in saying 'I bet' so the agent is going to do something in believing that he will do it, then one must suppose that his expression of purpose expresses belief and in consequence is propositional.

There are, however, a class of sentences which like expressions of purpose express something but which don't, except indirectly, express beliefs, viz. orders and expressions of wishes.

Where someone says 'Oh to be in England!' or 'Shut the door' he is expressing a wish, and in the latter case by giving a command, seeing to its realization. In these cases one could say that he is telling us what he wants, and compare them with an expression of purpose wherein the agent tells us what he has decided. But what distinguishes the latter from the former expressions is that he thinks he is telling us what he will do. When the time comes round for him to act, and he does act in the way he expressly intended, he can say to us 'You see — I did do what I said I would do'. This is precisely the way in which predictions are verified. Nothing like this could be said of expressions of wishes. At most one could say 'What I said I wanted has come about' or 'You have done what I told you to do'. These are not statements about verification.

Perhaps we can bring out the significance of this argument more clearly by referring back to the performative 'I promise'. After I have done what I promised to do by using this performative, I can also say 'You see — I did what I said I would do'. This, however, does not show that the performative 'I promise that, etc.', is propositional. The reason is that I did make the promise whether I did do what I said I would do or not. The *speech* act was something more than an announcement of what I would do. In the case of the expression of purpose likewise I do not merely tell you what I will or what I think I will do. I also form an intention. But the forming or having an intention is not a *speech* act over and above the telling you what I will do in the way that the promising is. Therefore there is absolutely no ground for saying that the expression of purpose is not propositional. The most one could say is that the intending is something more than the believing in the proposition.

The disinclination to call an expression of purpose propositional in spite of its difference from these non-propositional or supposedly non-propositional sentences is due simply to forgetfulness of the far-reaching distinction between predictions represented by 'I am going to, etc.', and 'He is going to, etc.', respectively. The multiplicity of ways in which an expression of purpose was shown to be confutable arose from indiscriminately lumping together confutation from different points of view. From the agent's point of view all these forms of confutation fall into order and only one is primary. He is faced implicitly or explicitly with the question for decision 'What am I going to do the circumstances being such-and-such?' to which he may answer implicitly or explicitly 'I am going to do such-and-such' or 'I am not going to do such-and-such'. These two answers are contradictory expressions of purpose, and in the context of the practical question 'What am I going to do the circumstances being such-and-such?' the one is the direct and primary confutation of the other. Other forms of confutation are directed towards questioning the validity of the practical question — not the validity of any one of its answers as compared with any one of the rest. Theoretical as well as practical questions are subject to this form of confutation (e.g. 'Is the present King of France bald?'). Consequently there are no grounds here for querying the propositional nature of the practical answers to practical questions.

It is true of course that seldom would an agent say of two contradictory answers to a practical question that the one is true and the other false. But the reasons for his disinclination do not bear the construction that expressions of purpose are not propositional. One reason is that 'true' and 'false' are adjectives whereby one appraises propositions that lie before one for consideration. Now this is hardly the relation in which the agent finds himself with respect to his expressions of purpose. The only sort of appraisal which he can make of an expression of purpose must be implicit in his expression of purpose. Perhaps, however, there are circumstances in which he would say 'It is true that I am going to, etc.', or 'It is false that I am going to, etc.', e.g. where another person has been speculating in his presence about what the agent is going to do. In this case the total expression is the expression of purpose of the agent, and the prediction which he appraises is specified as the other person's prediction. But appraisal of his own expression of purpose is not a function which falls within the agent's standpoint as such.

Another reason for not using 'true' and 'false' of expressions of purpose confronts us in the view that these adjectives indicate correspondence with the facts, whatever that means. No prediction, however, corresponds or fails to correspond with the facts except in a retrospective sense, since the event predicted hasn't yet occurred or failed to occur. They certainly don't correspond in the sense in which 'The sun is now shining' may or may not correspond with facts. Perhaps, however, we mean something analogous, viz. that the event will occur as predicted. But if so, why shouldn't this be said of expressions of purpose, viz. that what they say will happen will happen?

Alternatively, perhaps we mean that there are sufficient inductive grounds at the moment of prediction for supposing that the event will turn out as predicted. Hampshire seems to have something like this in mind when he denies[1] that expressions of purpose are predictions. I agree to the extent that expressions of purpose are not inductive conclusions, and that they are not based on inductively sufficient grounds. But if this is to be taken as a sufficient reason for denying the predictiveness of such expressions, it requires as a premiss that the actual futurity of an event consists in a present sufficiency of inductive grounds. So long as the sufficiency of inductive grounds and the futurity of the event are allowed to be logically independent there can be no good reason for denying predictive status to an expression of purpose just because it is necessarily deficient in inductive grounds. To propose a definition of futurity in terms of a sufficiency of inductive grounds seems, however, to be circular. It defines the statement 'X will happen' in terms of itself as meaning 'There are sufficient inductive grounds at the moment for supposing that X will happen'. There may be ways of trying to avoid this circularity, but I don't propose to follow them out, since in Chapter ix I shall show that futurity consists contrariwise of the necessary insufficiency of causal determinants and hence of inductive grounds.

It is only when we turn from the agent to the alien who assesses the agent's expression of purpose that we can say that this expression is directly confutable in more than one way. The alien can challenge the authenticity of an expression of purpose where it would be irrelevant for the agent to do so. The agent as such is concerned purely with the question 'What am I going to do?' and whatever answer he gives to that is the answer, since the question is addressed primarily to himself, though of course he may deceive others about the answer he gives or the question by which he was faced. Again the alien can challenge the part which the agent's sincerity actually will play in bringing about the action

[1] See *Thought and Action*, pp. 104ff.

on the grounds that the objective conditions won't work towards the action in quite the way which the agent thinks. But once again it can only be from the alien point of view that the objective conditions and the subjective conditions consisting of the agent's intention can be regarded as possessing a certain degree of independence from each other, for the agent's decision is formed in consideration of what he takes the objective conditions to be.

All in all, then, we have seen on the negative side that expressions of purpose do not resemble those supposedly non-propositional locutions to which they can most plausibly be assimilated more than they resemble propositions. On the positive side we have found that the apparent parity of the widely disparate form of confutation to which they are subject is reduceable to order by means of the distinction between the two standpoints. It is only from the alien standpoint that the factual method of confuting the agent's expression of purpose by means of a contradictory prediction fails to meet the expression of purpose head on as it were. This is solely because the predictions of aliens and agents don't enjoy the same logical status.

Fuller development of the more positive claims of expressions of purpose to propositional status will have to be left to later chapters. What these in effect will show is that the tendency to treat all indicative sentences as if they were propositional has not been the most pernicious legacy from our philosophical past. More pernicious still has been the tendency to regard the indicative mood as having some sort of ontological priority. The most significant feature of an Indeterministic Libertarian ontology is that it transfers this priority to the interrogative mood. The philosophy of logical atomism is now almost universally decried, but its central failing has never yet been properly exposed. It regards reality as essentially determinate, and only determinable or questionable from an epistemological point of view, i.e. relative to a purely contingent ignorance. As opposed to this, Libertarianism makes reality essentially determinable, and it is through practical knowledge and the practical question 'What am I going to do?' that we are immediately aware of this. In the technical terms of logical atomism the disjunctive 'or' is not primarily a truth-functional constant. Its use is ontologically basic for making the determinableness of reality fully explicit, and where it is used in this way the propositions which it can disjoin have an entirely different status from propositions which can be disjoined truth-functionally alone. All criticism of logical atomism which fails to presuppose the essentially interrogative constitution of reality is useless, for unless reality is essentially determinable logical atomism must be true.

The second lacuna in the argument of the previous sections consisted in my apparent willingness to assume that from the alien point of view the going to do something consists in the existence of complete conditions in the present of that thing coming about. I may seem to have accepted, then, that the alien point of view is essentially deterministic. If one accepts this, however, one must suppose there to be a fundamental contradiction between the agent's and the alien's standpoint towards the agent. One must suppose that a man must think that the actions which he intends at the moment are incompletely conditioned, but that his past intentional actions or the actions of others at any time are by contrast completely conditioned. There is no strict self-contradiction here of course, since it is a contradiction between two different standpoints, but when one remembers that the agent can occupy both standpoints towards his action, even if not simultaneously, the contradiction seems undesirable. It seems intolerable to suppose that the agent must in principle continually recant ontological beliefs which he has inevitably held the moment before.

This suggests that the alien standpoint need not be quite so deterministic as I appeared to entertain at the outset, and that once we understand how different an expression of purpose is from an alien prediction of the same action this understanding reacts in turn on our understanding of the alien's prediction. We must remember that the alien standpoint is just as practical as the agent's since it is the point of view of the other agent who has to make up his mind how to act in consideration of circumstances which include the agent as perhaps their most important constituent. One can only form a firm intention in so far as the circumstances are stable and predictable. One must be able to tell what will happen if one acts in one way as distinct from what will happen if one acts in another. The assurance with which one plans for the future depends upon the assurance with which one judges the causal potentialities of one's situation. Hence the standpoint of any agent whether towards others or towards himself must comprise, though in varying ways, a relative Determinism which sets the limits within which choice is open and articulate.

However, the standpoint of the alien consists not merely of the standpoint of an agent towards his circumstances in their relatively impersonal aspect. In this aspect there is no difference between the two standpoints as we have delimited them. All agents have to consider their circumstances. What makes a standpoint alien is the fact that the circumstances which it considers comprises other agents whose possible actions have to be taken into account. We have now to ask ourselves whether even the relative degree of Determinism peculiar to any agent towards his circumstances in their more impersonal aspect must likewise be peculiar to the alien whose outlook is by definition towards the specifically personal aspect. Must the alien in fact treat the agent's purposive belief as an event which in conjunction with the physical and possibly other psychological circumstances completes the causal antecedents of the action?

If he must, he wouldn't necessarily be interpreting the agent's action deterministically. He could always postulate some indeterminately conditioning factor antecedent to the supervening intention. The intention on this interpretation would be an indispensable causal condition of the action but would itself have no complete antecedent causal condition. However, our immediate problem is not simply to save the hypothesis of Indeterminism but to save it in a manner reconcilable with the indeterminacy presupposed by the agent's standpoint. We have failed entirely to explain why the alien should interpolate some occult cause between the antecedent indeterminately conditioning factor and the action which the agent is about to do, where in contrast the agent's ontology leaves no room for any such extra. We can remove this anomaly by an analysis of the concept of intention solely in terms of the essential and most obvious difference between the two standpoints.

What distinguishes the one standpoint from the other is its different and incompatible relation to the circumstances of action. At any given moment there is a set of purely physical circumstances more or less common to a number of agents — a lowest common denominator as it were. Each agent to the extent to which he can plan for the future must believe that his circumstances are sufficiently clear cut in their causal potentialities to give scope to and to delimit the possibilities of action in a specific and determinate way. Circumstances can be defined as purely physical where this assumption is most fully justified. They act as a sort of fulcrum for choice. Over and above the purely physical or impersonal part of the agent's circumstances there are, however, other agents, and this is the source of the incompatibility.

The agent has to reckon with these and their actions so far as possible in the same way as he reckons with the circumstances in their purely impersonal aspect. There is, however, an important disparity. He must to begin with recognize that others have in their future actions a scope similar to that which he allows to his own. Secondly, he must recognize that each of the others may include any other agent as a circumstance to be reckoned with in a way in which the agent cannot include himself. This last is the source of the incompatibility. Everybody has to adopt the standpoint of the agent in respect of some project however unambitious. In doing so he must ascribe to himself the initiative in delimiting the scope of action enjoyed by other agents. Their freedom to choose between a number of specific actions is contingent upon his permission or submission or co-operation or restraint or constraint, and he looks upon himself as free to exercise or withhold these forms of influence. In believing this he adopts towards the others the alien point of view.

The reason, then, why the notion of intention enters into the alien but not the agent's standpoint is simply that it signifies the qualified nature of the scope of activity within which the agent from the alien standpoint is free to act. From the alien point of view the agent retains his indeterminate future but precisely what falls within this range of indeterminacy depends upon the alien or yet other agents. To say, then, that an action is intentional is not to say it has been conditioned by some sort of first cause which intervenes in time between the antecedent indeterminately conditioning factor and the intentional action. It simply indicates the qualified character of the agent's indeterminacy. Accordingly, the two standpoints are incompatible not because the one implies indeterminacy where the other does not. They are incompatible because the indeterminacy which both imply is implied as applying in different ways.

We can now review the conclusions of this chapter and show how they take their place in my argument as a whole in its present phase. In Chapter v we distinguished two main categories of process, viz. phenomena and activities. While in the majority of cases any process can be subsumed under either, the notion of responsibility or efficacy in the narrative sense is involved by the latter alone. We can speak indifferently of a sunset taking place or of the sun setting, but only in the latter case can we speak of something doing something. Responsibility, then, is possessed by things that do things, by substances and not by events. At the same time we took note that the category of activity applies to other things besides voluntary action, but that the agent is held responsible in the full narrative sense for voluntary action alone. What is the crucial distinction here? What does the setting of the sun or the flight of a stone lack to make them in the full sense actions of these objects? This is the question to which the negative and the positive conclusions of this chapter provide an answer.

Deficiencies in the two dominant analyses of voluntariness, i.e. analyses in terms of mental events or Rylean dispositions, have become obvious. One cannot satisfactorily analyse a voluntary action into a sequence of one-one causally connected events one of which must consist of the mental event we call volition. Neither can one analyse it into a one-one causally connected series of non-mental events the subsequent parts of which would have turned out differently in certain specific ways if the antecedent parts had likewise been different in certain ways. Both these analyses have been ruled out by the negative conclusion of this chapter, which is of even more general significance. It has ruled out all analyses of voluntary action in terms of one-one causal connections between successive events as inconsistent with voluntariness. Instead it demands a limited indeterminacy in the outcome of any situation where voluntary action must take place. Voluntary actions, accordingly, are constituted by one-many causal connections and for this reason come under the category of self-determining process specified in Chapter v. But now this category applies to events as specific instead of to events as bearers of certain general characteristics examples of which were cited there from the field of biology and history.

My positive conclusion, on the other hand, that expressions of purpose have a propositional content of unique logical status gives application to another broad category specified in Chapter v, viz. prospective process. In this way the categories of self-determining and prospective process have become associated, and we shall see in Chapter IX that this association amounts to logical identity. We have distinguished between two ways in which the sentence frame ' ... going to ... ' should be understood. Either the first person singular 'I', or some word with the same force, is indispensable towards completing its sense, or it is not. Where it is indispensable in this way, the sort of futurity or aboutness which the completed sentence indicates is just what constitutes the prospectiveness of prospective process. This sort of futurity is the peculiar preoccupation of expressions of purpose.

It is true, of course, that there are predictions of the form ' ... going to ... ' in which the 'I' is not indispensable even when it occurs, since somebody else could insert 'He' and make an equivalent prediction of the same logical status. These predictions seem to permit, even where they do not demand, that the aboutness or futurity of the event predicted be cashed in terms of present events, or more accurately events up to the present, which constitute sufficient conditions. But this sort of futurity is obviously derivative. How do we distinguish the fact that the stone has broken the window from the fact that it is about to break the window? Not simply through a sufficiency of antecedent causal conditions, but through the further fact that these antecedent conditions occurred some time back in the past instead of having just occurred. In other words the distinction depends upon the distinction between what at the moment is past and what is future being already available to us. The next two chapters will show in greater detail just how these depersonalized predictions are subsidiary to and derivative from expressions of purpose.

Just one further point. These conclusions may seem to have been based solely upon an analysis of our more reflective voluntary actions, viz. those which involve purpose, decision, and intention. Some of our voluntary actions, however, are not reflective, and yet we are responsible for them. Have I not, then, left

H

an important type of responsibility out of consideration? The answer is 'No' for two reasons. First, I showed in Chapter II, section 2, how unreflective voluntary action could be defined negatively in terms of intentions. Second, in this chapter I have been dealing not so much with intentions, purposes, etc., as with what those attitudes make explicit. They differ from other voluntary states simply in degree of self-awareness. But the object of awareness is common to the explicit and the inexplicit states.

CHAPTER VIII

THINGS AND PERSONS

Our main efforts have been directed so far towards the divorce of certain concepts. No divorce, however, is satisfactory without some settlement between the divorced parties, and up to the moment our interest in this has been somewhat marginal. Let us take, then, our principal distinction. What is the relation between the explanatory and the narrative types of responsibility? A whole cluster of more or less equivalent or subordinate questions arises from this one. What is the relation as well as the distinction between a voluntary action and the other events which it accompanies? What is the distinction and relation between a means and an end or between what we do for its own sake and what we do for the sake of something else? What is the distinction and relation between a mere thing and a person? This last formulation of the problem is perhaps suggested more directly by the preceding chapters than the others. We have succeeded in distinguishing processes in which things as such are engaged from processes which are the voluntary actions of agents, but have indicated only vaguely how they work together. Accordingly we can best explore the whole nexus of related problems by working towards the solution of this particular one.

I

In acting, the agent has to solve questions which are specific applications of the questions I have raised above. He cannot entertain a reasonable hope of realizing his intentions unless they have been formed in consideration of the circumstances, i.e. the objects surrounding him, and their previous behaviour. It is advisable, however, before going further to recognize a variety of types of voluntary action according to the role which consciousness plays in them.

One type consists of deliberate actions where considerable reflection may take place about the nature of the circumstances in which the agent is called to act prior to his forming a definite intention. This sort of action is more likely to take place where the circumstances are novel, e.g. when we plan an expedition. A second type consists of one type of habitual action. I make a decision, e.g. to walk home, and then carry it out, taking all the necessary turnings while all the time giving my attention to something entirely different. As a third type we have a controlled type of activity where execution follows recognition of the circumstances too closely for any process of deliberation to intervene, and where the circumstances are too novel for the response to be in any way habitual. A dog runs in front of my car and I brake practically instantaneously. I conduct a conversation with somebody and respond intelligently without any reflection. This type of action has been thought to require a behaviouristic analysis of voluntariness. There are two types of behaviouristic programme. One consists of an analysis of consciousness as such: the other consists of the whittling down of the role of consciousness in human behaviour. Behaviourists or their critics sometimes superimpose these two programmes rather indiscriminately upon each other. While I support neither I am here criticizing one application of the second alone. The vividness of one's experience during an activity like braking a car seems to me too outstanding for such an account to be plausible. The experience is odd, perhaps, for those who rely on neat distinctions between cognitions and conations, but none the less quite unmistakable. Certainly I don't reflect that there is a dog and that at my present speed it is likely to be hurt. I apprehend the dog immediately as not to be hurt and act accordingly. (The brake-applying mechanism is of course a conditioned reflex which rather complicates this example.) My mode of consciousness is gerundive in nature. One doesn't always apprehend the circumstances in purely descriptive categories and then imagine a course of action adapted to its descriptive qualities. One frequently apprehends the object immediately as requiring such-and-such an action.[1] Again, in the conduct of a conversation, I immediately apprehend the remark of the other person as requiring a particular answer in the same moment as I apprehend its meaning; or in making a speech I apprehend what I have just said as requiring such-and-such a conclusion without any process of reflection intervening. As a fourth type we have

[1] See F. H. Bradley, *Collected Essays*, vol. ii, pp. 39, 504, 505.

another kind of voluntary action where reflection, positive intention, or gerundive apprehension may all be absent. The process of breathing or of blinking is up to a point voluntary for we can stop it at least for short periods. Now normally when I breathe I don't deliberate about the necessity of breathing in order to live, nor do I do it merely out of habit, nor do I apprehend the situation immediately as requiring breathing, nor have I any positive intention to breathe. My action, however, is voluntary because it doesn't conflict with any of my other positive intentions, and the fact that it doesn't conflict with these intentions is an indispensable condition of its taking place. If, for instance, I found that my breathing interfered with my hearing a very slight noise, I could and would stop breathing in order to listen better. This type of action also has been subjected to behaviouristic misinterpretation. The undoubted fact that no positive intention or conscious idea is involved in the action does not mean that no intention is involved in the action. Finally, we have another type of habitual action. This is similar to such actions as breathing or blinking in the absence of positive intention, but it is dissimilar in having been formed by habit. I may have acquired the habit of switching off the electric light whenever I leave the room and may continue to do so even when it promotes no particular end of mine, such as the saving of expense. The action is voluntary because as soon as it became inconsistent with any of my ends I could desist. Is it possible, however, that there may be a further dissimilarity between this type of action and the fourth type exemplified by breathing. When I pass the electric switch possibly there may always be the gerundive feeling that it is to be pushed up.

I think this classification does sufficient justice to the various types of voluntary action. Diverse as they are, none of them invites a behaviouristic analysis. All of them involve consciousness more or less directly and this consciousness is at its most explicit in fully deliberate actions. Accordingly, we can confine our attention to deliberate actions in order to determine the relation between things and persons both from the alien and from the agent's standpoint.

Deliberation is sometimes conceived as taking one or both of two forms. Its alleged object is either to answer the question 'What is my end?' or the question 'How should I attain my end?'

The answer to the second question is supposed to presuppose the answer to the first, and the answer to the first to be independent of the answer to the second.

Certain deterministic accounts of deliberation seem particularly dependent on this conception. Deliberation, of course, always has been a challenge to the ingenuity of the Determinist, since the agent seems to entertain therein alternative actions as equally within his power or causally unsettled. The Determinist can take the short way with this and suppose that the agent is subject to an inescapable form of illusion. In doing so he finds himself in the quandary of one whose practical and theoretical postulates must always conflict. He must believe from the theoretical point of view that the laws of human nature determine all agents, including himself, to believe from the practical point of view that no laws are in operation where on the contrary some are. Alternatively he may try to restore consistency with his theoretical postulate by diminishing the claim of the practical.

One way of doing this is to distinguish between the two questions. According to this account questions of ends never present the agent with any great difficulty. His ends announce themselves, possibly after a certain amount of inner turmoil which like giddiness time often settles. In some cases they don't even announce themselves before going into operation, but work from under cover. Deliberation is confined to the process of deciding how to bring these ends about. Alternative courses are equally in his power in the sense that his belief that one of these would terminate in his end is a sufficient condition of his initiating that particular course.

Historically speaking, of course, there is no clear-cut line of division between Determinists and Libertarians on just how deliberation takes place. This has had a vitiating effect on the historical development of Libertarian doctrine. The view that deliberation centres round the solution to two distinct questions, about ends and means respectively, in which the latter has precedence over the former, has its origin in Aristotle's doctrine of the practical syllogism: and he on other counts is unmistakably Libertarian. This doctrine is rather more complex than the deterministic account of deliberation outlined above. It contains the more essential features of the latter account but modifies its deterministic implications in the most pernicious manner by means of the notion of weakness of will.

The practical syllogism consists of a major premiss specifying a state of affairs as desirable, a minor premiss specifying something as either an instance or cause of the desirable state, and finally an action, instead of a proposition, which follows validly or invalidly as conclusion. The major premiss is concerned with the question of the agent's end and this end according to Aristotle is not at issue at the moment of action. It is determined by his character which is the result of his previous moral education, and this is the only sense in which it is described as deliberate or chosen. The minor premiss is concerned with the question of the means to the agent's end. It alone is the conclusion to a process of deliberation in which alternative courses of action can accurately be described as at issue immediately before the moment of action. But the issue is primarily a theoretical one and determined by the theoretical discovery that one course alone will lead to the agent's precise predetermined end.

As an account of deliberate choice all this is definitely deterministic. But according to Aristotle once the choice about ends and means is made the appropriate action doesn't necessarily follow. Syllogistically speaking, it is possible for him to act irrationally or invalidly, and this is weakness of will. Now if we remember that for Aristotle the will is a first cause, it appears that its function resides not in the agent's capacity to exercise one or other form of choice, but in his capacity to syllogize practically or exercise strength of will. In this way the volitional phenomenon of strength and weakness of will has been promoted to an undeserved prominence in the history of philosophy. It is only one volitional phenomenon among others of equal importance. Weakness of will consists simply of inconstancy of purpose where the grounds for the original decision have undergone no relevant change. This inconstancy is usually instigated by discomfort of some sort or its more vivid anticipation. Accordingly, the occasion for weakness arises specifically where the choice lies between two or more courses, one of which alone is considered to lead to immediate preponderating discomfort. Where the latter condition does not hold, inconstancy of purpose is described as capricious rather than weak.

From this analysis it can be seen that there are many other occasions for intentional action in which strength or weakness of will is in no way involved. Now Aristotle has at least retained some sort of distinction between weakness of will and other forms of choice, though he overreaches himself by making will power a quite separate phenomenon from choice. Later Libertarians, however, have wanted to identify the function of will as first cause with the function of choice. As a result, every instance of choosing is considered to be an exercise of will power in which the will either beats or fails to beat down certain refractory desires which rebel against a relatively supine moral character or habit. Where there is no psychological conflict of this sort there can be no exercise of choice except upon means. In short, through this identification of will power with the exercise of choice the pernicious influence of the causal interpretation of willing has become confirmed among Libertarians and Determinists alike.

The purpose of this digression has been to show the fundamental importance of a correct account of deliberation in its relation to ends and means. Actually the formation of decisions about ends and means constitute only a rather special type of deliberation. In general, deliberation is concerned with the formation of intentions, and only in more specific though numerically preponderating instances with the distinction between ends and means, which is internal to intention. In these cases the decision to take something as an end is always correlative to and inseparable from the decision to take something else as a means.

It is perfectly true that if we could visualize a state of affairs as an end without having any idea how it could be brought about, then of logical necessity the answer to the question 'What is my end?' would precede the answer to the question how it is to be brought about. But this initial assumption is totally unjustified. In deliberation we quite frequently indeed visualize a state of affairs which appears intrinsically desirable, and only then consider the question how it is to be brought about. Here by 'intrinsically desirable' I do not mean, however, 'something one would desire even though nothing else existed'. I find the hypothesis of myself and a peach existing in a universal vacuum unappetizing as well as intellectually bemusing. It is enough if we mean that what is intrinsically desirable adds by its presence to the value for us of *most* situations. Even supposing then we visualize a state of affairs as intrinsically desirable, we cannot confer upon it the status of end or something we aim at, until we find a solution, or a number of solutions, to the question how to bring it about. We cannot even predict that once we have found the solution to bringing it about we would aim at it as an end, unless we have some previous idea what the solution is likely to be.

In the first place, as will be readily agreed, it is not until we are assured that the question 'How?' has some answer that the intrinsically desirable state of affairs can be made an end. If we discovered that it was beyond our power to bring it about in any form, we obviously could not continue to entertain it as an end. In the second place, even if we are satisfied that the intrinsically desirable state of affairs can be attained we still have to decide whether the method of attainment would make it worth while. What is for intrinsic reasons desirable may be for extrinsic reasons undesirable. By using any method of attainment we have to tolerate certain intrinsically undesirable states of affairs and relinquish yet other intrinsically desirable states of affairs. We can perfect our command of a musical instrument, for instance, only by long hours of laborious practice which could have been spent in the enjoyment of something else. In the third place, some of the methods of attainment may be themselves more or less intrinsically desirable. The expatriate, for instance, may consider whether to go home on leave by plane or boat, and opt for the sea journey because it is pleasanter though less quick. Here it may well be that one wouldn't make any journey at all unless one wished to go home on leave, but yet the journey is found intrinsically desirable.

Whether one is a Libertarian or a Determinist one must, then, recognize that deliberation is monolithic. Ends only become determinate for the agent in the course of considering the causal properties of the circumstances in which he is called upon to act. The circumstances consist basically of physical objects with various causal potentialities and we form our ends, or our ends become formed, only in the course of discovering the various ways in which the causal potentialities of these objects can be realized. Even the differentiation of our sensuality into the basic appetites must depend upon insight into the physical peculiarities of our bodies which are the most basic part of our circumstances. It is unlikely, for instance, that the female praying-mantis, given consciousness, would recognize precisely the same distinction between hunger and the sex urge as we do, since she has a physio-logical compulsion to satisfy the first whenever she satisfies the second. Likewise, to turn to less sensual ends, the ambitious politician may not at first be aware of the relative value he attaches to popularity as distinct from personal integrity or the welfare of his country. He becomes aware of the two as distinct, and his own personal equation between them, solely from the experience that one must be subordinated to the other in circumstances which do not permit him to aim at both.

It is worth while to establish the monolithic nature of deliberation and to clarify the relation between circumstances and the formation of purpose through an analysis of more specific examples. Let us make a preliminary distinction between single-step and multiple-step actions. Certain objects or aims can be attained by a direct or comparatively direct action, but others only in consequence of a chain of successive actions each with a more immediate object attained for the sake of the later objects. In the single-step action the causal dispositions of the immediate circumstances at the moment of action are sufficient to define the range of mutually exclusive possibilities for the future, one of which is the agent's object. In the multiple-step action the immediate causal dispositions are merely sufficient to define a range of mutually exclusive possibilities for the future, at least one of which possesses a disposition which defines at more or less remote removes a range of mutually exclusive possibilities in one of which the agent's object can be attained.

The following is an example of what is roughly speaking a single-step action, and is designed to show that a relatively simple action may involve a complex process of deliberation. A team of engineers at work in Florida find the humid heat unbearably oppressive. The grass around is thick and parched. They set it on fire. Convection currents funnel the vapour into the cooler atmosphere above. Condensation in the form of a thunder-storm ensues, and the downpour cools the lower atmosphere. Atmospheric humidity is also reduced and they can once more perspire freely.

Now probably they have to souse the grass liberally with kerosene before setting it alight: and probably they have to kindle separate fires over an extensive area at adequately spaced intervals to ensure convection in sufficient volume. Probably, therefore, the action involves more than one stage. But if we ignore these preliminaries our example still illustrates a natural uncontrived complexity confined to one step. The components of this complex are the causal or instrumental dispositions inhering in the circumstances which the engineers exploit. These dispositions can be expressed in hypothetical propositions roughly as follows: if it will rain it will become cooler; if this vapour condenses it will rain; if convection in sufficient volume occurs the vapour will condense; if fire covers a certain area convection in sufficient volume will occur; if this grass is kindled the requisite conflagration will develop. As a contributory chain we can add: if when working we perspire freely we keep moderately cool; if atmospheric humidity lowers we perspire freely when working; if condensation occurs atmospheric humidity will lower; if convection occurs condensation will occur.

This analysis makes it clear that the total circumstances for the engineers form a close-knit nexus of instrumental dispositions which as an ordered unit can be comprehensively described as the disposition to cool. This disposition can be expressed by a chain of statements about the necessary one-one or many-one connections between events. The nexus is close-knit because, provided the circumstances specified are taken as forming a closed system, the exploitation of the combustibility of the grass leads inevitably to the exploitation of the remaining elementary dispositions comprising the complex disposition. Of course, if we do not regard the circumstances as a closed system, we can conceive of additional circumstances in which the original chain-reaction could be interrupted. The detonation of an atomic charge, for instance, in the locality of the fire half-way through the chain-reaction could no doubt puff the impending thunderstorm into non-existence.

Now the close-knit nexus we have examined is disclosed to the agent through his deliberation, and illustrates how he can only form his ends in the course of such deliberation. No doubt the discomfort of humid heat was felt by the engineers before their insight. That, however, does not confer the status of an end or aim upon the removal of the discomfort. They might, after all, have gained some relief by knocking-off for the day. If so, the fact that they didn't shows that their object was more complex. Physical relief could not compensate for the loss of time or money entailed by this method. Likewise their decision to exploit the close-knit nexus of dispositions would entail decisions about what to tolerate and what to relinquish and what to regard as compensating this tolerance or sacrifice. The possibility of such decision, or understanding of one's will, would depend upon a clear understanding of the component dispositions. Many of the consequences of lighting the grass might have been listed as intrinsically or extrinsically undesirable: e.g. the devastation of a large area of vegetation possibly serving other useful purposes, the wholesale and painful destruction of innocuous local fauna, the sudden flooding caused by the deluge, mud, and other attendant evils, which we cannot fully enumerate without a more detailed knowledge of the situation. On the credit side we must not forget to place the successful execution of a bright idea or exercise of engineering ingenuity, which would give the process as a whole an intrinsic value. The mere fact that the action involved a fairly detailed insight into the dispositional properties of the circumstances would of itself provide an incentive for exploiting them. It is even possible that no special attention or weight was given to the physical discomfort before the insight supervened.

The temptation to suppose that objects of action become determinate before insight into the circumstances in which they are to be realized possibly arises from a failure to distinguish clearly between purpose and wish. It is perfectly true that our wishes, as distinct from our purposes, can be highly determinate even where we have little regard for our actual circumstances. This is simply because they are the substance of our day-dreams. Our wishes have a tendency to be idle. When they are determinate what makes them wishes and what makes them idle is that the circumstances, if any, which they visualize are not the real circumstances and have little likelihood of becoming the real circumstances. Thus the party of engineers may have conjured up severally in the moment of their discomfort visions of long cool drinks in their favourite bars or drug-stores back home. The object of their wish is indeed determinate, but it is entirely imaginary and un-realizable. Wishes, however, need not be entirely idle. They have a practical role in the genesis of multiple-step actions in which circumstances which are not real can be made real as the result of action. Nevertheless, where this is possible, it is because the wish is wholly determinate neither in itself nor in the circumstances to which it extends; for only thus can it be adapted to the real circumstances.

Let us now turn to the sort of complexity found in multiple-step actions. Here the agent exploits the instrumental dispositions of the circumstances in order to develop modified circumstances with more highly specialized instrumental dispositions in which he can act on later occasions. The construction of the sort of article for which it is conventional to reserve the terms 'instrument', 'tool', 'utensil', etc., affords one type of instance, though not the only one, of such action.

The following is admittedly a fictitious reconstruction of pre-history. Let us suppose that the same palaeolithic agent made his flint tools with which he made his flint weapons with which he hunted. The action taken by this huntsman-cum-craftsman-armourer in shooting a deer, for instance, is a multiple-step action. In contrast to our previous example, such an action owes its complexity to a loosely knit nexus of instrumental dispositions related serially in degree of specialization. It is loosely knit because the exploitation of the antecedent instrumental dispositions does not involve inevitable exploitation of the subsequent dispositions in the nexus. The intervention of the agent is required at each stage. Although each component disposition has to be exploited in a fairly determinate way in order to become a member of just that nexus and no other, at each stage there is no compulsion that it should be exploited in precisely that fairly determinate way, apart from the agent's determination that it should become a member of just that nexus.

It is equally clear in the instance of multiple-step actions that decisions to tolerate, sacrifice, and take in compensation, depend upon insight into the complex of instrumental dispositions inherent in the circumstances. The very project of slaying a deer cannot be formed by our primitive agent until it is apprehended as vulnerable-to-skilled-use-of-manufactured-missile. Prior to the manufacture of such missiles and the acquisition of skill in their use the slaying of deer could only be regarded as the outcome of a lucky fluke and not as a practical project. Then, even after it can be entertained as an end, the agent has yet to consider whether it is worth all the labour of first making tools to make weapons and then of acquiring skill in the use of these weapons. Might it not be better to bask in the sun and, when the pangs of hunger became pressing, to collect roots, worms, and grubs?

On the other hand we must not ignore the possibility that the instrumental processes have, or come to have, an intrinsic value for the agent. First, they may have the positive value peculiar to any exercise of a highly articulate and complex choice. Such choices give the agent a feeling of mastery over his environment. The more instruments at his disposal the greater the number of possibilities from which he can pick his end. Then again, we might reasonably expect our palaeolithic agent to derive from his composite activity as a whole the peculiar satisfaction which in modern times the butcher, the toxophilist, and the craftsman-armourer can, if they have a sense of vocation, only experience in part.

Living as we do in a technological age where superficially the prevailing motives are profit and, perhaps, leisure, we tend to ignore the intrinsic value of instrumental choices. Instrumental processes consume time and labour. This is inimical both to profit and leisure. Cost of production is one of the limits to profit. Hence the profit motive must lead to the pruning of the instrumental process down to the minimum. By the profit and leisure criteria the instrumental process is worse than intrinsically worthless, and consequently is in need of extrinsic justification. Paradoxically, profit and leisure as objects of action can be attained in ideal form only when nothing has been done for their sake. Hence the incentive to technological advance and the cutting down of instrumental process to the minimum. We must regard the increasing variety of sports and hobbies as the compensating social phenomenon. To a large extent they are the debris left in the wake of techno-logical advance. In them there persist in fossilized form the old techniques which are no longer of instrumental value. Yachting, hiking, fencing, etc., were all at one time under less genteel names highly practical and necessary occupations, but now have been cut adrift from their former ends by the development of new techniques with the same purpose. The fact that they are still practised shows that they had an intrinsic value which perhaps has become clearly distinguishable from that of their ends only after they have become obsolete as techniques.

I am not, of course, trying to obliterate the distinction between means and end altogether, but merely pointing out that it is justified in any one of four main situations. First, one part of an action may be of intrinsic positive value for the agent, and another part may be intrinsically indifferent in value or, apart from its causal connection with the former, extrinsically indifferent. Second, one part of an action may be of intrinsic positive value for the agent and another part intrinsically bad or, apart from its causal connection with the former, extrinsically bad. Third, one part of an action may be of intrinsic positive value for the agent in such a way that in the circumstances the agent would accept no substitute for it, and another part may be likewise of intrinsic positive value, but in such a way that the agent would dispense with it, if it precluded the first part. In all three cases we distinguish the first part from the other part as an end from a means. Fourth, a general characteristic of an action may have intrinsic positive value for the agent and he may have no preference for one of its specific forms rather than another. In this case the distinction between ends and means coincides with the distinction between the general and the specific. Finally, we must not forget the situation in which the means-ends distinction is entirely inapplicable. Every part of the action may be of equal value to the agent. The complete activity can, of course, be described as an end provided we no longer use that word as strictly correlative to 'means'. Sporting activities perhaps approximate most closely to this type of action. We must also notice that there are situations intermediate to these four main types.

This classification of means-end relationships leans rather heavily on a notion which, of course, we cannot take for granted, viz. intrinsic value or desirablity. I have been using 'value' and 'desirability', interchangeably and both in their psychological non-ethical sense, to indicate the disposition to arouse desire in the agent. On the other hand, I have distinguished between this notion and that of end in an equally psychological sense. My point has been that an intrinsically valuable state will be endowed by the agent with the status of end in the sort of situations listed above, but that this can be done only in the course of considering the causal possibilities of the situation in which he finds himself with a view to finding whether they include situations of this sort. But where does this knowledge of intrinsic desirability come from? Must we suppose that the agent approaches every particular situation which calls for action, if not with a preformed list of ends, at least with some such list of general desires arranged in order of attractive power? Is the process of deliberation about causal possibilities simply a process of putting the attractive forces which happen to be applicable to the given situation into gear, as it were, so that their objects thereby become ends and motivate the agent?

We must admit that it is natural and customary to talk in this way of desires spurring us to action, of conflicts of motives within us, and so on. And once we find ourselves talking in this way extensions to the mechanistic model become equally natural. We have to explain, for instance, why the law of composition of forces seems not to apply to action. Why is the immobility of Buridan's ass comical rather than commonplace? Simply, we must infer, because built into the psychological mechanism there is a force known as 'will'. This force is designed for the purpose among others of preventing mutual frustration among conflicting desires by, where necessary, intervening on behalf of one, or alternatively for rescuing the maxim 'Ought implies can' by backing the sense of duty when it is threatened by stronger desires.

There is not the slightest need, however, for this mechanistic apparatus. Desires like ends are just as articulate as the circumstances allow them to be. There is no preordained list. They become distinct only as soon as the possibility that they are capable of independent satisfaction becomes understood. Their relative independence from each other does not consist in some sort of isolation from other recurrent features in a man's environment, but simply in the variability of the circumstances which accompany their objects on different occasions and are at the same time enhanced thereby.

The agent isn't confined in his deliberation just to a consideration of the particular circumstances at hand. He may form intentions of the sort that can be realized not merely in the situation on one given occasion, but in a variety of situations on a variety of occasions. There will be, then, a variable and a constant element in his intention which makes it capable of fulfilment in its variable aspect in a limited variety of ways, and in its constant aspect in one way only but on an indefinite number of occasions. This relative constancy and variability may be formed only in the course of reviewing past performances in the same limited variety of circumstances, but the actual dispensation between the two aspects can only occur as a matter of more or less deliberate policy. The possible number and organization of the constant elements is determined entirely by the limits to the variety of the different sorts of situation that are causally possible, and by the agent's insight into these. The supposed conflict of desires consists simply of the agent's doubt over which of two conflicting dispensations between constant and variable elements to put afoot where both are applicable to his present situation.

Perhaps this analysis can best be explained schematically. Supposing the agent decides to do an action AB, then this action can only be said to be motivated by the desire for A where the agent would on the same occasion have been prepared, had the circumstances permitted only AC, to perform AC. This willingness indicates that there is a constant element in the agent's intention consisting of A, and a variable element permitting both B and C as its values. In most cases, of course, the dispensation between the two elements within the intention is voluntary rather than itself fully intentional. In other words, the interchangeability of B and C as values for the variable is (a) not contrary to the agent's intention, and (b) the fact that it is not contrary to the agent's intention is an indispensable condition of their being interchangeable.

A man may be equally willing to take tea or coffee depending on which is available on specific occasions. Before we can say that his motive is a desire to quench his thirst we have to be satisfied that he is willing in a fairly deliberate way to take anything so long as it is wet, not unpalatable, and perhaps fairly harmless. Otherwise all we are entitled to say is that on the occasion when he was offered tea he desired to drink tea, and on the occasion when offered coffee he desired to drink coffee. Where thirst is his

I

motive, however, his indifference to the precise nature of the beverage need not be consciously explicit. It need only be true that, had he been offered tea instead of the coffee he actually was offered, his taking the tea would not have been contrary to any of his intentions, and that this fact would have been an indispensable condition of his taking the tea.

The main point of this section has been the comparatively simple one that decisions are made in consideration of the instrumental potentialities of the circumstances. From the agent's standpoint the circumstances are actually constitutive of what he is going to do. From the alien point of view the relation is slightly less direct, since what the agent's circumstances are and what he thinks they are need not entirely coincide. Accordingly, from the alien standpoint it is what the agent *takes* to be the circumstances that are constitutive of his *decision*. This relatively simple point has been complicated by the necessity to distinguish between means and ends. Questions of means and questions of ends are distinguishable. It is, however, a mistake to identify the practical question what to do as dealing primarily with decision about ends and to suppose that decision about means follows on thereafter. This is perhaps the result of confusing decisions made by committees with decisions made by agents. Committees quite frequently reach certain agreements about what directives are to be sent to their technical experts who deal with the question how these directives are to be implemented. The directives, however, are usually issued in the faith, frequently unjustified, that the technical experts are competent to devise means of implementation. Relative then to the committee which issues the directives the technical experts are the factors whose limitations have to be taken into consideration in deciding what directives to give, and, in any case, quite frequently technical experts are asked to report back before a final directive is issued.

In the course of elucidating the complications introduced by the means-end distinction we became involved with the mechanistic conception of decision as a sort of football-cum-referee of the desires. This muddle stems directly from supposing that deliberation about means is only consequent upon deliberation about ends. Deliberation, on the contrary, is monolithic. The distinction of means from ends arises simply from the fact that in specific situations which call for action most human beings are capable of visualizing alternative situations and of reaching decisions which are meant to apply to all these situations when or if they arise. Understood in this way the distinction clarifies other aspects of action besides deliberation. I shall indicate briefly its relevance to two of these before passing on to other topics.

In the first place the distinction is one of the more important sources of the subjective impression that time passes more or less quickly. Due to the variability of the circumstances in which the same intention can be realized, it can be realized more or less quickly. In this respect human action has properties analogous to the 'plasticity' displayed by the behaviour of certain organisms which we have considered in Chapter v. Both kinds of behaviour, then, can be brought under the category of temporally indefinite process. If we simply formed, and executed successfully, intentions with no means-end organization our lives would have the uniform pace of one damned thing after another.

In the second place it is through the means-end organization of the agent's intentions that the alien can predict his future actions in a way that doesn't presuppose them completely determined by antecedent causal conditions. Through this organization the agent's intention becomes applicable to other situations besides his present one. It thus becomes possible for the alien, having observed in the past on various occasions the circumstances in which the agent has acted in various ways, to gauge which variations in circumstances yet to come will prove consistent with the variable element in which of the intentions manifested by the agent on these past occasions. It is in fact through this relationship that we can form a truer conception of moral character than the dreary conformist conception of character as habit supplied by Aristotle.

2

We have next to consider whether this internal or constitutive relation of circumstances to action or things to persons is as unique as I may seem to be representing. One may argue that the potentialities for the future of inanimate objects as well are constituted by other objects animate or inanimate that surround them. Hence their aboutness to do something is likewise constituted by these objects. The potentialities of a hammer, for instance, are constituted by the potentialities of the nail, or, to revert to a former example, the potentialities of a stone are constituted by the potentialities of a window-pane. To describe these relations it is convenient to distinguish between active and passive potentialities. Each respective kind requires the existence of the other. The potentiality of the hammer to hammer in requires the existence of such things as nails with the potentiality of being hammered in. The potentialities of the human body are determined in this way as well. Those of the hand, for instance, are greatly increased by the creation of such instruments as hammers and nails. It is because of these constitutive relations between the potentialities of objects that several substances can become involved in the activity of one substance, or the process relative to which that substance is the agent. For instance, it is in this way that the window is involved in the activity of the stone breaking it.

The analogy between the potentialities of objects or things as such and the potentialities of agents is of course illuminating, but must remain misleading so long as we fail to detect an essential distinction. This distinction has been sufficiently familiar since noted by Aristotle in *Metaphysics*, 1019^{b}, 20-35, and can be identified in contemporary idiom as the contrast between dispositions or tendencies (Rylean variety), on the one hand, and causal possibilities, on the other. Thus the potentialities common to agents and things consist of dispositions to behave in certain ways, whereas those peculiar to agents alone consist merely of causal possibilities. Simple though it may seem there has been among contemporary philosophers a fairly consistent failure to make this distinction. The cause of this has been their preoccupation with the words 'can' and 'could have' which are common to the discussion both of dispositions and possibilities. Even in criticizing this failure, however, it is possible to fall into error as I have done elsewhere.[1] The mistake I made was to class dispositions as generically distinct from causal possibilities, whereas as I shall show in a moment they are merely a subspecies.

Causal possibility is closely analogous to logical possibility. To say ' "*p*" is possible' is equivalent to saying ' "*p*" is not necessarily false', and this equivalence holds whether the two modalities of possibility are logical or causal. Thus 'That there is life on Mars is causally possible' is equivalent to 'That there is life on Mars is not by causal necessity false'. Where we use words which express causal possibility we withhold our assent from an inference that something is false.

Statements referring to dispositions *ipso facto* refer to possibilities. Thus 'Grass can burn' or 'He can swim' mean 'It is not causally necessary that grass never burns' and 'It is not causally necessary that he never swims' respectively. In general, statements about dispositions state that some rule is not a rule of causal necessity. The generality of such statements, of course, is usually contingent upon certain relatively permanent or standing conditions. For instance, one may accept 'Grass can burn' as true only in the dry season. This explains why dispositions can be acquired and lost. Again, from the chemist's point of view diamonds are soluble, whereas from the layman's they are insoluble. This is because the standing conditions which are standard for the former, i.e. his skill and laboratory materials, are not likewise standard for the latter.

It is clear from this analysis, then, that 'can', etc., refer to possibilities even in disposition-statements. The difference between possibilities and dispositions lies in the difference between two sorts of reason which may be given against some sort of rule as a rule of necessity. One may think (*a*) that there are no applicable rules of causal necessity except the second-order rule to this effect, or (*b*) that some contrary rule of causal necessity is applicable. In either case one must subscribe to the truth of some hypothetical statement of the form 'if … then … ' In case (*a*) one believes that if the situation is such-and-such then no rules of causal necessity are applicable to the occurrence of a given event. In case (*b*) one denies, for instance, that glass by rule of causal necessity never breaks on the strength of the contrary rule that if under certain standard conditions it is given a sharp knock then it will break. In either case, however, the reasons belong to the contextual implications of the use of 'can' and do not form part of the analysis.

It is here that contemporary analyses of the use of 'can' have gone wrong. The mistake is a double one consisting, first in supposing that (*b*) specifies the only sort of circumstances to which the use of 'can' and its appropriate variants are applicable, and second in supposing that what (b) specifies is an analysis. Thus according to Ryle[1] 'To say that this lump of sugar is soluble is to say it would dissolve, if submerged anywhere, at any time and in any parcel of water'. In fact it doesn't say anything so specific, but simply that it is not causally necessary for sugar never to dissolve, on a basis such as that which Ryle specifies in his supposed analysis. Oddly enough Ryle himself seems to recognize this, for later[2] he gives the same sort of analysis as the one I have just given. He writes:

> To say that something can be the case does not entail that it is the case, or, of course, that it is in suspense between being and not being the case, but only that there is no license to infer from something else, specified or unspecified, to its not being the case.

This unexceptionable statement, however, doesn't deter him from supposing that 'can' and its appropriate variants are used solely for the purpose of referring to dispositions.

The mistake has serious consequences when Ryle and those who follow him turn to the analysis of voluntary action. One criterion of voluntary action to which he pays particular attention[3] is expressed in the form 'He could have helped doing it'. Ryle interprets this as a disposition possessed by the agent, and since we say this sort of thing only about intelligent beings, he identifies the disposition with the particular sort which he calls 'a know-how'. Thus he interprets the sentence as saying 'He knew how to help doing it'. From this he draws the rather revisionary conclusion that only mistakes or errors are properly described as voluntary, since he thinks that it is only of erroneous conduct that one could sensibly ask whether the agent knew how to help doing it.

I have dealt with the details of Ryle's argument more thoroughly elsewhere.[4] It is enough here to have drawn the distinction between causal possibility and causal dispositions: for the full weight of Ryle's case depends upon supposing that such guarantors of voluntary action as 'He could have helped doing it' refer univocally to dispositions. He is confirmed in this assumption simply by his failure to distinguish any other kind of 'could have'.

---

[1] *The Concept of Mind*, p. 123.   [2] Op. cit., p. 127.
[3] Op. cit., pp. 69ff.   [4] Op. cit.

Other writers have made the same mistake in a rather different way. Ryle's argument depends upon supposing, first, that where the auxiliaries 'can', etc., are used in discussing voluntary action they refer to know-hows or skills, and then that references to know-hows are analysable into hypotheticals. The others rush rather more precipitately into analysis into hypotheticals. 'I (he) can' is analysed[1] into 'I (he) will, if I (he) choose(s)' or into various variants of this which can be derived by substituting 'will', 'intend', 'decide', 'desire', 'want', 'try', etc., in place of 'choose'. The mistake here is basically the same as Ryle's but deserves further attention because in some ways it is more misleading.

The peril consists in the analysis being roughly correct but invariably misinterpreted. If in deliberating about what to do I find that I can do either of two things though not both, it seems reasonable to infer that I will do the one if I choose, and also the other if I choose. The inference seems to hold in the converse direction as well. But what right have we, in taking the modal and hypothetical statements as equivalent, to suppose that either refers to a disposition? What right have we, in other words, to suppose that the 'if' clause lays down a causal condition?

In a slightly dissimilar context Austin writes:[2]

The dictionary tells us that the word from which our *if* is descended expressed, or even meant, 'doubt' or 'hesitation' or 'condition' or 'stipulation'. Of these 'condition' has been given a prodigious innings by grammarians, lexicographers, and philosophers alike: it is time for 'doubt' and 'hesitation' to be remembered.

This is at least suggestive even though its accent of authority seems to carry no precise sense. Just how different or just how similar the four mentioned functions may be or in what circumstances one is exhibited rather than the rest remains a matter for interpretation. Austin believes that in the locution 'I can, if I choose' or 'I could have, if I had chosen' doubt or hesitation are prominent. When he turns to 'I shall, if I choose' he thinks stipu-

---

[1] Cf. G. E. Moore, *Ethics*, chap. vi; R. E. Hobart, 'Free Will as Involving Determinism and Inconceivable without it', *Mind*, January 1934; P. F. Nowell-Smith, *Ethics*, p. 278.
[2] *Ifs and Cans* (British Academy lecture, 1956), p. 114.

lation is more in the forefront. He says[1] 'the point to notice is that "I shall" is not an assertion of *fact* but an expression of *intention*, verging towards the giving of an undertaking: and the "*if*", consequently, is the *if* not of condition but of stipulation'. Pursuing this line he argues that 'I shall marry him, if I choose to' is rather like 'I intend to marry him if I choose' which in turn is rather like 'I promise to marry him if he will have me'. He concludes, therefore, that the *if*-clause belongs to the content of the undertaking and does not qualify the fact of the undertaking being given.

As against this I have already argued in the previous chapter that expressions of intention are not, nor even verge towards, the giving of undertakings. They are not performative — at least not in any direct way. Quite apart from this, however, there is something very odd about interpreting the clause 'if I choose' as similar in force *mutatis mutandis* to 'if he will have me' in his last example. Just what sort of stipulation could this be? If you give an undertaking by saying 'I shall marry him', just what modification do you proceed to make in what you undertake by adding 'if I choose'? So far from modifying it, or making a stipulation in what you have undertaken, you seem in fact to be withdrawing all appearance of having given an undertaking. A still more serious criticism of Austin's analysis is that it is too limited in scope, since undertakings of this sort are made mainly in the first person. Now 'He will if he chooses' seems to me to be no more vacuous as a statement than 'I shall if I choose', and the *if*-clause seems to have a similar function: yet it seems to give no further undertaking than is ordinarily given by any hypothetical prediction. Consequently, whatever the significant difference between a condition and a stipulation may be, it seems inapplicable to our present problem.

The mistake to my mind does not lie so much in interpreting the *if*-clause as expressing a condition rather than a stipulation or doubt as in interpreting it as laying down a *causal* condition. Where one says 'I shall if I choose' or 'He will if he chooses' normally one simply is saying that there is a choice before the agent. One may also be saying something slightly stronger, supposing the 'if' has also the force of 'only if', as it has in stipulations of a less special kind than Austin's: one may be saying that if the agent

[1] Op. cit., p. 116.

does the action in question it is done as a matter of choice. The point here, which the phrase 'there is a choice' emphasizes more successfully, is that the *if*-clause indicates the sort of happening which the action, if it occurs will be, viz. a voluntary happening. Instead of laying down a causal condition of a psychological sort it classifies the action ontologically as lacking complete causal determination. Perhaps after all, then, we could say that the *if*-clause expresses something like doubt, viz. that the occurrence of the action is *in question* in the ontological sense supplied by the notion of causal indeterminacy.

The *if*-clause may, of course, have certain rather more special-ized though connected functions depending upon the context and in some cases upon the grammatical person. For instance, where somebody says 'I shall if I choose' he may be saying something like 'Leave it to me — it's my responsibility, not yours', and a similar analysis applies for the third person variant. Again, if he says in the third person 'He will if he chooses' he may wish to indicate that the agent has the opportunity to do the action, though possibly he may not realize this. Here it seems to me the *if*-clause does assume specifically a psychological significance. It indicates that there is a psychological condition to the agent's doing the action, viz. that he realizes that he has the opportunity to do it. If we are to follow out our preceding chapter in its findings on the alien point of view, even this condition must not be interpreted as causal.

It seems that in the use of 'can' we have to recognize distinc-tions in logical status which are the exact parallel of the distinc-tions in the use of the predictive sentence-frame ' ... going to ... ' The use of 'can' indicates the presence of alternative ways of filling the latter half of this frame in. But the precise logical status of the frame even when semi-completed in this way depends upon whether the former half is filled in by 'I' to make an expression of purpose or by 'He' as in the alien's prediction of the agent's action. Hence the 'can' in 'I can' must to this extent have a different logical status from the 'can' in 'He can'. The difference lies in the emergence of intention in the alien point of view as a factor with which the alien must reckon in predicting the agent's action. From the agent's point of view nothing of this sort stands between the circumstances of the action and his being about to perform it.

Now, because of this intervening factor consisting of the agent's intention, choice, or decision, the agent's ability to take any one of a number of courses must have a rather more complex constitution from the alien point of view than from the agent's. For the agent it is constituted entirely by what we have conveniently called the circumstances. For the alien it is only constituted by these same circumstances plus the agent's ability to choose within the limits which the circumstances permit. For this reason 'He will if he chooses' can be accepted as an analysis of 'He can' even where the *if*-clause is interpreted as laying down a psychological condition instead of being interpreted to indicate the existence of indeterminacy or choice in a purely ontological sense. We have already argued, however, that it would be a mistake to interpret this psychological condition as specifying some sort of causal event. It indicates simply that from the alien point of view the limits within which the agent's indeterminacy falls is subordinate or subject to the alien's indeterminacy. The agent's freedom is as it were on feu from the alien or from others, in the sense that the scope of the manifold of possibilities before him is limited and controlled by the scope of the manifold of possibilities open to others. For this reason even though 'He will if he chooses' can be accepted as an analysis of 'He can', we mustn't interpret it as offering a dispositional analysis, even where the *if*-clause specifically lays down a psychological condition.

My main backing for refusing to interpret the proposed analysis of 'can' into the hypothetical form as concerned with dispositions in the commonly accepted sense has come so far from the results of the preceding chapters. I need not rely solely upon consistency, however, since there are good independent reasons for rejecting that interpretation. If we regard the *if*-clause as laying down an antecedent causal condition of the truth of the main clause, we induce a vicious circularity. Nobody chooses to perform an action unless he thinks he can do it. 'He chooses to do X' hence implies 'He thinks he can do X' and 'I choose to do X' seems to have the stronger implication 'I can do X'. If then we analyse 'He can' into 'He will if he chooses', this analysans implies 'He will if he thinks he can' which implies 'He will if he thinks he will if he thinks he will if ... ' and so on *ad infinitum*.

This seems to indicate that there is another way of qualifying a prediction than by laying down a causal condition of its being fulfilled, viz. by indicating that there are no conditions of it rather than something else being fulfilled. The function of the 'if' in the proposed analysis is to indicate that the prediction is qualified, while that of the verb 'to choose' is to indicate in which way it is qualified. Either we accept this conclusion or it is forced upon us the hard way: for if we regard the *if*-clause as laying down a causal condition the infinite regress which results impresses on us that the condition can never be complete.

We have, indeed, mentioned earlier different variants to the analysis of 'can' into hypotheticals, derived by substituting 'decide', or 'intend' or 'desire' or 'want' or 'try' in place of 'choose' in the *if*-clause. Perhaps it might be thought that these escape the regress which affects 'choose'. Closer examination shows, however, that they don't, with the exception of the variant which employs 'try'. The particular variant 'He will if he intends' also implies 'He will if he thinks he can', because it is logically impossible for anyone to intend to do what they think they are unable to do. Now this particular variant is implicit in all the rest, in so far as they supply an adequate analysis of 'can'. 'He will if he wants', for instance, only means the same as 'He can' provided the want is conceived as constituting an intention. If it is weaker than an intention it certainly does not follow from 'He can do X' that he will do X if he wants. In the case of 'He will if he tries' one has to admit that trying certainly does not imply thinking that one can. Hence there is no infinite regress involved by this variant. But this is the sole variant I cannot accept as providing a basis for the use of 'can'. 'He will if he tries' certainly does not follow from 'He can', for the agent may not try in the correct way.

For these reasons, then, one must not interpret the use of 'can' for the purpose of detailing alternatives which lie before the agent at the moment of action as indicative of dispositions in the sense commonly accepted among philosophers today. I may be accused, however, of oversimplifying the uses of 'can' which are relevant to voluntary action. Even if it is true that 'can' is used to indicate possibility there may be more than the two reasons which I have given for saying that something is causally possible.

For instance, I can take part in a certain conference for the reason that it takes place at the very time that I happen to be visiting the town in which it is held. On the other hand, I cannot take part for the reason that I lack the necessary qualifications, e.g. an up-to-date membership card of some association. Or again, I cannot take part for the reason that I lack the necessary know-how or professional competence to take part. Or again, I cannot because I don't think that the conference is taking place. Conversely it may be the case that I can take part because one or more of the last three reasons is incorrect, but cannot take part because I am never in the correct place at the time of the conference, or because the conference hasn't been organized. In short, before one can say without qualification of somebody that he can take part in the conference, or avoid taking part, in the sense that he has a choice of doing either, one has to satisfy oneself that he has a number of different sorts of ability. These consist first of the opportunity, secondly the qualifications, thirdly the competence, and fourthly the knowledge of the opportunity.

Among this plethora of 'cans', however, the degree of independence is not as great as may at first sight appear. They can be accounted for in terms of the distinctions we have already made with slight though important rectifications. There is in fact only one sense in which 'can' has been used throughout and only two reasons for applying it in that sense, viz. (a) the non-existence of a causal law determining the occurrence rather than the non-occurrence of an action, and (b) the existence of contrary laws to a proposed law that a certain action never happens. The relatively numerous ways in which, as we have discovered, 'can' is used in discussing an action is due first to these reasons being applicable within a narrower or wider context, and second to their being applicable to a particular or to a general situation.

Certain objective conditions such as a conference being held in the town visited by the agent can be classed as opportunity only relative to certain abilities which pertain to the agent. One says 'I had the opportunity to take part in the Bell Ringers' Annual Conference, if only I had been a member of the association at the time and had been able to ring bells'. Where it is indicated by the context either that one knows the agent to possess these abilities or that for the moment one is indifferent to this question, it is permissible on learning that the agent is in the town during the period of the conference to say 'He can take part in the conference

now'. Where the context does not indicate this, one is only entitled to say 'He can take part in the conference now, provided
that, etc. etc.' If the conditions which one here specifies are unfulfilled, it follows in the latter context and there alone that the agent
cannot take part. The fact, then, that in the same objective situation
one may sometimes say that he can and sometimes that he cannot
take part in the conference, doesn't in itself indicate different uses
or senses of the word 'can'. Here it is simply due to the reasons
for presuming possibility being applied within a wider or
narrower context.

It is true again that when we use 'can' to indicate that the agent
has a certain enablement such as a membership card, or that he
has an ability consisting in a know-how or professional competence, we are using 'can' for a different reason from the one which
led us to indicate opportunity. The agent possesses these abilities
irrespective of whether he has the opportunity or not, even
though he possesses the opportunity in the strictest application of
the word only if he possesses these abilities. The abilities are in
fact dispositions in a rather wider sense of that word than I have
so far allowed. The agent possesses these abilities generally in
virtue of the fact that it isn't necessarily the case that whatever the
occasion may be he won't take part in the conference. This, of
course, may be true of the agent even when it is said on occasions
which don't yield the opportunity to manifest the ability. Not all
abilities of this sort can be analysed on the Rylean model which
has been commonly accepted. The agent's ability consisting in
his having a membership card can indeed be analysed into hypotheticals of a causal kind. It can be said to consist of the fact that
if he presents his membership card to the secretary of the conference he will be granted permission to take part. The professional competence, however, does not permit this sort of analysis.
Generally speaking, it will follow under no sort of causal condition that the agent will actually take part even if he has the
opportunity. He may play a purely passive role and be indistin-
guishable from somebody with no competence at all. The most
that one can say is that he will take part if he chooses. But as we
have just seen, an *if*-clause of this sort does not indicate a causal
condition.

Consequently I must revise my analysis of the sense of 'can' in its causal application. It indicates possibility, but we have to distinguish two main ways in which it does this. In the first way it indicates the possibility of something occurring on a particular occasion which may not be possible on another occasion. In this first application it indicates opportunity within a wider or narrower context. In the second way it indicates the possibility of something happening on occasions of a certain sort without reference to any particular instance of this sort as in the first way. In this application it indicates a disposition, whereas in the first way it indicates, when used more strictly, that a disposition has application to a particular occasion or situation.

Now it is primarily in this second way that we must recognize the distinction between the two reasons I gave originally for applying the word 'can'. One may say that an object or agent has a disposition to behave in a certain way for the reason that one is satisfied that if certain causal conditions are fulfilled under certain standard conditions then the behaviour will result. On the other hand, one may be unable to give any reason of this sort. One may simply believe that it is not necessarily the case that the thing in question won't behave in that way, on the ground that there is no causal law determining whether under certain standard conditions the thing will or will not behave in that way. This is the sort of reason which we have when indicating skills or competences or know-hows ranging from something so elementary as picking one's nose to something as complex as contributing usefully to a conference.

One loose end to this discussion of 'cans' remains. I have reserved it to the present because it brings into play the distinction between standpoints once again. One condition of the agent's ability to act in a particular way on a particular occasion consists, we saw, in his believing that the objective conditions which constitute an opportunity for the action are as they in fact are. This condition like the agent's competence or know-how is a condition without which the objective conditions cannot be regarded as an opportunity in the fullest application. One says 'I had the opportunity to attend the conference if only I had known it'. It is, however, only from the alien point of view that one has to take account of what the agent believes in this way. It cannot without circularity enter as a distinguishable factor into the agent's point of view. To treat it as logically distinguishable for the agent is to suppose that I believe that in the fullest application of 'can' I can now do a specific action only if I find that I believe in the fullest application of 'can' that I can do the action now. If my belief includes itself as grounds in this way it must be circular, an obvious symptom of logical disease. The solution is to recognize the difference of status between 'can' with 'I' as subject and 'can' with 'He' as subject. We have already given an analysis of this difference.

The overall result of this section has been to show that the auxiliary 'can' and its associates are used to indicate possibilities with particular or general application. Where these possibilities are of the causal kind they may have two different sorts of basis, (a) the fact that no causal law is applicable relative to certain occurrences, and (b) the fact that the contrary to certain specific causal laws are applicable. Accordingly we must distinguish between two kinds of causal possibility. The kind which has a basis of type (a) seems to be peculiar to agents in the voluntary actions open to them on specific occasions, and in the sort of general ability, disposition, or know-how which only voluntary actions can manifest. This has been shown in part by our earlier analysis of intention as well as the present analysis of the use of 'can' in this context. The other type of causal possibility has a basis of type (b) and is common to all sorts of things including persons in so far as all these things possess dispositions which are not capable of being manifested solely by voluntary action.

My argument that causal possibility of the first type is peculiar to agents alone can become complete only in the next chapter. There is, however, one exception to this conclusion which we can note here. Even the Determinist can give application to the first kind of possibility, viz. where the evidence is not sufficiently specific to allow the application of any causal law. Thus he may permit the statement 'There may be life on Mars' simply on the grounds that there is no causal law relating to such unspecific conditions as there being life and being on Mars. However, it would perhaps be better to class the possibility here as epistemological rather than causal.

We are now in a position to complete the answer given by

section 1 to the problem set at the beginning of this chapter. In showing how persons are related to things we detected an analogous relation between things and things. But where does the analogy break down? Where does the relation between Prometheus and the fire differ from, say, the relation between the fire and the cauldron? Failure to distinguish between the two relations would be just another form of confusion between narrative and explanatory responsibility.

It is now evident that potentialities which are dispositions in the Rylean sense alone must be clearly distinguished from potentialities which are *bare* causal possibilities with a basis of type (*a*). The latter are peculiar to agents alone whereas the former are common both to agents and to other things. Thus the circumstances are constitutive of the dispositions of instruments, or objects which might conceivably become instruments, because they are the standing conditions under which given a certain antecedent a certain consequence will result. On the other hand, the circumstances are constitutive of the agent's potentialities, and what he is about to do, because they limit the scope of causal possibility or the courses between which he can choose by providing or failing to provide opportunities for the manifestation of his competence to do various sorts of things. They distinguish the choice open today from the choice open yesterday.

Correlative to the notion of potentiality there is the notion of substance, and consequently correlative to the two types of potentiality we must recognize two types of substance. An important reason why we regard a stone as an object rather than a continuum of events is that we wish to ascribe to it a possibility or disposition in virtue of which it may behave in ways different from the ways in which it actually does behave. We may describe it as dangerous even though it isn't actually knocking somebody's eye out. Obviously, then, the notion of substance has the function of relating two or more events together as bearing the relation of alternatives to each other. But why should we relate events in this way? Why shouldn't we instead follow Heraclitus or Russell in viewing events as what in Chapter v I have called phenomena rather than activities?

If the world was a deterministic world and we were omniscient there would be no point at all in grouping as alternatives to each other events which would have happened had certain antecedent events been different, together with events which actually do happen. Even were such a world logically possible there would be no causal possibility in it of antecedent events having been different from what they were except once again in the sense that had events antecedent to them been different then different events would have followed, and so on. We can simplify the argument by dividing any one causal chain or line within this deterministic world into two parts consisting of one event and all the others. Whether the others are antecedent or subsequent in time does not matter, since all events are *ex hypothesi* in one-one relation within the line. Within this causal partnership, then, the counterfactual hypothesis of the event being different from what it is supposes something causally possible only in the sense that the event would be different on the counterfactual hypothesis that the others are different. But this latter counterfactual only supposes what is causally possible in the sense that these other events would be different on the former counterfactual hypothesis that the event is different.

The only form of causal possibility applicable in these circumstances is, then, definable in terms of the *if-then* relationship and the notion of not being the case or counterfactuality. In this world the conception consisting of a group of events considered as alternatives must in consequence have application only through fantasy. The sole function which the notion of substance can serve is to indicate in what respects this world is like certain fantasy worlds, viz. in being governed by the same causal laws, and in what respects it is unlike others, viz. in not being governed by the same causal laws.

In a deterministic world in which we are not omniscient, in which, say, we know all the laws of the system but don't in all cases know how to fill in the variables, the notion of substance would have an epistemological justification. There is here a possibility of an event being different from what it is in a sense which is not dependent upon counterfactuality. In this sense a number of events are equally possible where our knowledge of their causal correlates is not sufficiently precise for it to be possible to deduce which event from a certain limited group are determined thereby. In this situation, however, the notion of

K

substance is no more than a convenience stemming from a human frailty.

It is only in an indeterministic world constituted by causal possibilities of type (*a*) that the notion of substance has metaphysical or ontological application. In this indeterministic world, provided it is not too indeterministic, the notion of substance has metaphysical application in two different ways. First, there is substance in the absolute or primary sense which consists in there being a number of occurrences which are alternatives in an equally absolute or primary sense. There is, in other words, no causal law which determines that in a specific situation one rather than another of the occurrences should occur. Second, there is substance in the relative or secondary sense. It consists in there being alternatives to an actual event once again in the sense that had the antecedent events been different the event would not have been actual. But now there is a genuine independent possibility that the antecedent events might have been different due to the presence of substance in the primary sense. Hence the metaphysical application of substance in the secondary sense depends upon its application in the primary sense.

In virtue of this relation substance in the secondary sense is constitutive of substance in the primary sense. Things and persons in what they have in common are constitutive of agents, not of course in a spatial sense of constitutive, but in the sense which I hope this chapter has elucidated.

CHAPTER IX

INDETERMINACY AND TIME ORDER

IN preceding chapters narrative has been distinguished from explanatory responsibility, and to a certain extent the connection between the two has been worked out. Each type of responsibility is associated with an entirely different form of prediction: for narrative responsibility pertains to voluntary action alone, voluntary action is necessarily associated more or less directly with intention, and the vehicle of intention consists of the uniquely personalized form of prediction to which the first person singular grammatical form is most appropriate. In Chapter VII we saw that this predictive form definitely implies indeterminacy in responsibility of the explanatory kind. It takes time, however, to assimilate conceptual demarcations of this sort. In particular it might still be thought that without a detailed explanation of *how* the agent proceeds from one action to the next, of *how* through his agency, choice, intention, etc., the future becomes determinate in one way rather than another, the main purpose of any account of action such as mine must remain unfulfilled.

To expect such an account here is, of course, to kick against the confines of the demarcations which I have elicited. No explanation of this sort ought to be asked for. But how do we fortify ourselves against the insistent incoherence of such mixed-metaphor feelings as that unless something pushes or pulls the future out of the womb of the past or present, time would remain in a state of permanent suspense like an incomplete stammer, or losing its forward thrust topple into some undifferentiated eternity? What we now need is a fuller analysis of temporal concepts. In what follows I shall show that temporal order and in particular the concepts of past, present, and future can be given meaning in terms of, or derived from the bare concept of indeterminacy. Not only does my being about to do something imply indeterminacy, but conversely indeterminacy implies the sort of personalized 'being about to' which is mine. This runs counter to Broad's argument[1] that Libertarian indeterminacy is

[1] See *Determinism, Indeterminism, and Libertarianism* (C.U.P.), reprinted in *Ethics and the History of Philosophy*.

most likely an indispensable condition, but very improbably a sufficient condition, of action or narrative responsibility. Thus we can dismiss our mixed-metaphor feelings as conceptual abortion rather than intuitive insight. This analysis at the same time confirms the conclusion of Chapter VII that the difference between expressions of purpose and other sorts of prediction doesn't consist in the latter alone being propositional, but that each refers to a state of affairs of radically different though related ontological structure.

I

In Chapter I we considered ways in which it seemed that a temporally successive series of events could be necessarily connected. But one assumption underlying our discussion was left unexamined. We assumed throughout that logically temporal order was quite independent of the necessary connections between events — that one event can succeed another irrespective of whether the connection is one-one, many-one, or one-many. To decide, for instance, whether the necessary connection between referent and relatum was one-many or many-one, we determined whether the singular term preceded or succeeded the plural term in time. But if the asymmetry of temporal order depends instead upon the asymmetry of the relation of singularity to plurality among the necessarily connected terms, then the distinction between one-many and many-one necessary connections is no longer legitimate. It can only be sustained where the events are incompletely characterized, as earlier we suggested that they are in, for instance, teleological explanations of organic behaviour.

In the present chapter the assumption of logical independence will be explicitly rejected. We shall derive the temporal order with its unique differentiation into past, present, and future directly from Libertarian indeterminacy in a suitably revised sense of that notion. Accordingly, the voluntary action which I am about to do not only depends for its voluntary nature on a certain causal independence from antecedents but at the same time acquires its character of aboutness or futurity from this same causal independence or indeterminacy. It follows further that this characteristic of aboutness can require no type of explanation that is incompatible with Libertarian indeterminacy.

If we regard some sort of temporal order as more ultimate than the necessary connection between events, it is indeed possible to give accounts of the dating function[1] of the present which are perfectly consistent with Determinism. Fault may be found with them on other grounds, but as accounts of the dating function peculiar to the present in what I have called prospective process they seem adequate. Their basic assumption is that events are in relations of before and after in a timeless sense of the verb 'are'. Temporal order is thus basically undated, but one can, it is supposed, account for the distinction between past and future in terms of the relationship of one particular series among concurrent series of events to the other series of events with which the former is concurrent. This privileged series according to one account[2] is the series of my utterances written or spoken: according to another[3] it is the series of my cognitive states. According to the first 'A was before B' means that A is (timeless copula) before B and that also A is (timeless copula) before this particular utterance of the sentence. According to the second, the sentence means that A is (timeless copula) before B and that also A is (timeless copula) before the cognitive state expressed by the utterance. Likewise, according to the first account, 'A will be before B' means that A is (timeless copula) before B and that A is (timeless copula) after the utterance. According to the second 'A will be before B' means that A is (timeless copula) before B and that A is (timeless copula) after the cognitive state expressed by the utterance.

Both theories give what is apparently an adequate account of one temporal characteristic, viz. that the temporal order of events is directly or indirectly related by our more colloquial modes of speech to one moment of time which we call 'the present'. Furthermore, they appear to explain why this date though variable is not determined by arbitrary selection. The fact that I describe the battle of Hastings in the past rather than the future tense for instance is not a matter of subjective choice. One event in the temporal series does not perform the dating function as well as any other. According to the one theory, what dates the serial relation between two events can only be the utterance of

[1] Cf. Chapter III.
[2] E.g. Reichenbach, *Elements of Logic*, chap. 7, section 51. Cf. L. Jonathan Cohen, 'Tense Usage and Propositions' (*Analysis*, vol. II, no. 4, 1951) for a more refined version.
[3] E.g. A. J. Ayer, 'Statements about the Past', *Ar. Soc. Proc., 1951-52*

some proposition about them. Once we make an utterance the dating event is determined by a logical necessity. According to the other theory, the dating event is the cognition of the temporally ordered events and is likewise determined by logical necessity.

It is not my intention here to enter into the deficiencies of these theories — they are indeed considerable — but simply to develop the alternative Libertarian account. This denies that all events that ever have occurred or ever will occur are (timeless copula) in any sort of temporal relation to each other. Or more accurately, it denies that the timeless copula has a legitimate use in this connection. Instead it provides through the indeterministic hypothesis a relation whereby one can derive a serial order which has essentially the nature of serial order in general and then consider in greater detail what characterizes temporal order in particular.

It is customary to regard any particular serial order of a set of terms as relative to some specific relation which holds between the terms, and acts as their ordering principle. I do not wish to depart from this analysis so much as to qualify a certain interpretation of it.

Russell has written:[1]

> We must not look for the definition of order in the nature of the set of terms to be ordered, since the set of terms has many orders. The order lies not in the *class* of terms, but in the relation among the members of the class, in respect of which some appear as earlier and some as later. The fact that a class may have orders is due to the fact that there can be many relations holding among the members of one single class.

In this way he introduces the question raised in his next sentence, viz. 'What properties must a relation have in order to give rise to an order?' and I propose to give his answer — with which I am largely in agreement — before returning to criticize the above quotation.

The properties of an ordering relation are three. It must be asymmetrical, transitive, and connected. The relation *father of*, for instance, possesses asymmetry because if X is father of Y, Y cannot be father of X. On the other hand, it is not a transitive

---

[1] *Introduction to Mathematical Philosophy*, pp. 30-1.

relation, because, although Y may be in turn father of Z, X is not father but grandfather of Z. We have to go to the more generic relation of *ancestor of* to find an instance of transitivity. To define the property of being connected I reproduce Russell's definitions of three more elementary concepts, viz. that of the domain, converse domain, and field of a relation, respectively. The applicability of these definitions appears, it is true, to be restricted to dyadic relations; but once this is appreciated, the modifications which would give these definitions greater universality are sufficiently obvious and for my present purpose can safely be ignored.

> The *domain* of a relation consists of those terms that have the relation to something or other, and the *converse domain* consists of all those terms to which something or other has the relation ... *The field* of the relation consists of its domain and its converse domain together.[1]

And this leads to the following definition of 'connected':

> A relation is *connected* when, given any two different terms of its field, the relation holds between the first and the second, or between the second and the first (not excluding the possibility that both may happen, though both cannot happen if the relation is asymmetrical).[2]

It will be observed that *ancestor of*, though both asymmetrical and transitive, is not connected, because it contains parents and siblings.

From this analysis of serial order it is apparent that the same set of terms may belong to the field of a number of relations which may possess all three of the properties just specified. Consequently the same set of terms may possess a number of entirely different orders. Let us take, for instance, a number of flashes of coloured light, no two of which are the same in intensity, saturation, or duration. It is possible to serialize this set in accordance with any one of the three relations *intenser than, more saturated than, longer than*; and no one of the series thus derived need coincide with another.

¹ Op. cit., p. 32.   ² Ibid.

Now does Russell's analysis of serial order apply to temporal order as well? Is, for instance, the temporal order of the set of flashes likewise dependent upon a relation? If so, upon what relation? And is this relation just one among a number of relations such as those already specified: or is it in some sense more fundamental to the set than these?

In the face of such questions as these we must reconsider our initial quotation from Russell — in particular the statement that 'order lies not in the *class* of terms but in the relation among the members of the class'. If we accept the latter part of this statement (i.e. that order lies in a relation among the members of a class) as applicable to temporal order, must we accept the former half as well (that order lies not in the class of terms)? There seem strong reasons for not doing so.

The temporal order of a set of events seems inseparable from that set taken as a set of particular actual individual events. I do not deny that the same set of events may have very different orders according to the relation that one selects. I merely aver that if the temporal order depends upon a relation, that relation, and that relation alone, must be basic to the existence of the set or sets of things which actually happen. Here, I suppose, I am struggling towards one facet of the truism that temporal order is the order in which events *come to be* or occur,[1] although to link this order with a relation is more than a truism. This relation, one must emphasize, should be basic to the *existence* of the members of the set as *individuals*, and not to the properties which these individuals possess.

The set of light flashes may serve to establish this point. It might conceivably have an exact replica in another set such that both sets correspond exactly in the intensity, saturation, and duration of their members. Now no matter how complete the correspondence between members of the two sets may be in these and *any other characteristics*, it remains perfectly possible for the temporal order of the members in one set to be quite different in that set from the temporal order of their exact replicas in the other set. Again, we might take a set of events which were exactly similar in all their characteristics. If the temporal order depended

[1] Cf. C. D. Broad's penetrating study of time in *Scientific Thought*, pp. 65ff, and *Examination of McTaggart's Philosophy*, p. 280 passim.

upon relations in respect of any of the characteristics which they can have in common with each other all the members of this set would accordingly be simultaneous with each other. But there seems to be no logical necessity for instances of any common characteristic or set of characteristics to be simultaneous. Another indication of the same fact is that when we are given that a number of events have occurred, we have to rely upon observation to determine the order in which they have occurred. We can never derive the order solely from a complete knowledge of their characteristics, independently of inductively established causal laws. Accordingly, temporal order is basic to the existence of events as individually distinct from each other rather than as instances of certain characteristics.

Russell's account of serial order requires modification in one part. But what about the second part of his statement? Is it true that like other orders temporal order lies in a relation between the terms that are temporally ordered? To some the difference between it and other orders may seem sufficiently great not to justify in the instance of the one what is justified in that of the others. They might consider that temporal order is unique or *sui generis* (to use a stock formula for philosophical deflation). Temporal order would be the ultimate relation between events and not derived from something more ultimate. The attraction of such a theory, however, is one of despair at finding a more fundamental relation. Two facts have to be explained:

(*a*) the present has a dating function, and is not arbitrarily selected from other moments in time to fulfil this function;

(*b*) temporal order is basic to the existence of events as individual things.

If we find an explanation of these two facts, the attraction of the *sui generis* account will become less urgent. Without further delay I shall show how Libertarianism supplies the solution required.

2

The indeterminacy postulated by Libertarianism can no longer be regarded as *in the first place* a relation between events. In Chapter IV I fell short of showing that the one-many or stage-by-stage structure peculiar to process was essentially constitutive

of events, because I gave the relation terms which were themselves events. Now I shall show that terms exist as events, and as
things occupying a temporal position, only through this relation.
For this purpose a diagram of the following kind will prove useful.
Each of the points here represents a thing which is not *in the first
place* an event, but only an event when taken in the relationships
represented by the lines. These lines do not represent anything
in time which could be regarded as analogous to length in space
(e.g. duration). Consequently, I cannot be accused of spatializing
time except in the rather trivial sense in which any diagram spatia-
lizes what it represents. The diagram has been employed solely

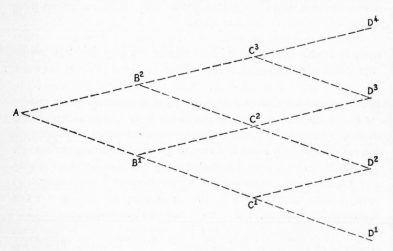

for its synoptic virtues; it can and will be interpreted in entirely
non-spatial concepts. It is a rather more serious matter that the
diagram represents a very special case of the type of interrelation-
ship which I wish to examine. The tendency of the lines to diverge
towards the right predominates, but nevertheless some of them
do converge. The convergence could be avoided altogether in a
less compact diagram but only through sacrificing some of the
present diagram's synoptic virtues. I prefer, for the present
chapter, simply to ignore the convergent relation towards the
right and to examine the divergent relation alone. In the next
chapter I shall correct the serious inaccuracies thus entailed.

   This one-many relationship, then, is such that, in terms of the diagram, A entails and is entailed by the complete and exhaustive disjunction B^1 or B^2, B^1 entails and is entailed by the complete and exhaustive disjunction C^2 or C^3, and so on. To say B^1 or B^2 is a complete and exhaustive disjunction is here taken to mean that B^1 and B^2 are possible, that only B^1 and B^2 are possible and that in addition they are incompatible. Furthermore, the relation is taken as primarily between B^1 and B^2 rather than between propositions about their existence. The notions of necessity and possibility involved are not of the logical kind. I here take them as primitive notions which can acquire fuller definition from their consequences alone.

Now it will be observed that where we take A as having determinate existence the complete and exhaustive disjunction B must have indeterminate existence — for indeterminate existence I take by definition to consist of equal possibilities and the incompatible elements of B are both equally possible. For similar reasons the triplet C and the quadruplet D must have an indeterminate existence as well. There must in fact be three different orders of indeterminate existence depending upon whether the group is the B, C, or D group. One can represent these relations differently by saying that where A has existence, any basic element of B has merely possibility of existence of the first order, any basic element of C has merely possibility of existence of the second order and any basic element of D has merely possibility of existence of the third order. Now let us turn to the significance of this pattern of relationships.

It will be noticed that between the groups A, B, C, and D we have an asymmetrical, transitive, connected relation. The relations can be described as 'having members of a higher order of indeterminacy or mere possibility than'. Accordingly, we can arrange these groups in such an order that A comes first, B second, C third and D fourth. A further significant feature is that this order is basic to the existence of the individual members of these four groups. It is an order of possibility of existence with actual existence serving as a limit of this order. Accordingly, we have constructed a relation from which an order can be derived possessing at least one of the distinctive characteristics of temporal series, viz. that listed at the end of section 1 above as (*b*).

Let us now turn to the characteristic (*a*), viz. to the dating function of the present and the distinction between past and future. A similar distinction is also called for in the interrelated set which we have constructed. We began by taking A as having actual determinate existence, and the mode of existence of all the other terms was determined by this postulate. But what happens if we take another postulate and confer actual determinate existence upon, say, B^1 instead of A? When we do this the set of interrelated terms immediately becomes divisible into two sets. One set consists of the terms which are entailed by but do not entail B^1, and the other set consists of the terms which both entail and are entailed by B^1. Thus A is entailed by but does not entail B^1. Accordingly, if we postulate that B^1 has determinate actual existence, we must likewise suppose that A has determinate existence. Again, the disjunction C^1 or C^2 and the disjunction of D^1 or D^2 and D^2 or D^3 both entail and are entailed by B^1. Accordingly, relative to B^1 each of the individual elements of these disjunctions has in varying orders only possibility of existence.

This distinction between two distinct sets, with B^1 as their common origin, one of actual determinate existents and the other of possibilities, seems to correspond closely with the familiar distinction between past and future. In other respects the correspondence is equally close. For instance, we noted earlier that the distinction between past and future is not an arbitrary one depending upon whim. Now it may be objected that we constructed two sets from our set of interrelated terms simply by postulating in an entirely arbitrary manner that B^1 had actual determinate existence. But mightn't we have postulated with as much justification that any of the other terms within the same sets had actual determinate existence? The answer is 'no'. It is by a logical necessity that we must refer the relations between the serially ordered sets of terms to one of their number and no other.

Any set which comprehends determinate and disjunctive terms related in the way outlined is both self-determining and self-ordering. It possesses both these functions primarily through including one key term. This key term determines the precise constitution both of the determinate subset and of the subset of disjunctions which the set comprehends. Relative to the comprehensive set every other term which it includes is either too liberal or illiberal in what it permits to joint-membership. The key term accounts for the joint-membership of all, but only through their being related to each other in certain specific ways. For this reason, then, the set which it originates is both self-determining and self-ordering.

Thus B^1 rules out the following terms as possibilities of any order of existence, viz. C^3 and D^4. If in contrast we were to postulate C^1 as having actual determinate existence we would in addition rule out D^3 as having possibility of existence of any order. In other words the point at which the set of determinate existents divides from the set of indeterminate existents or the set of possibilities depends upon the precise membership of these sets. No other term in either of these sets could serve as the point of division without broadening or narrowing the membership of these sets. Therefore, within any set of terms it is not an arbitrary matter which term functions as the point of division between the two subsets.

Here lies the parallel between the series we have constructed and fact (*a*) about time. At any moment after 1815 it is (i.e. was or will be) true to say 'The battle of Hastings was before the battle of Waterloo', but before 1066 it could only have been true to say 'The battle of Hastings will be before the battle of Waterloo'. In short there is no absolute serial relation of any date or dated event to other dates or dated events in the temporal series. It is always relative to some other. In the same way there is no absolute order for any pair of terms in our set of disjunctive relationships, since whether they both belong to one set is relative to some other term. For this reason the terms exist as possibilities or actualities in the timeless sense of 'exist', only relative to the absolute origin A. Relative to other origins their existence as actualities or possibilities is not timeless. The distinctions made by the various past and future tenses in both the indicative and subjunctive moods become necessary.

If, then, the Libertarian hypothesis is correct, we may conclude that a temporally inflected language is something more than a convenient but dispensable linguistic device, as some have represented it. Likewise it is something more than a mode of description dictated by a purely contingent ignorance about the part of time we call 'the future', as others have believed. On the Libertarian theory the primary necessity for a temporally inflected language is neither linguistic nor epistemological, but ontological.

I have still to show, however, that temporal inflections have on the Libertarian hypothesis to be used in the manner peculiar to the standpoint of the agent as demonstrated in Chapter VII. From the agent's standpoint his immediate future is as determinate as his past, for it is in a prediction of the form 'I am going to ... ' that he expresses his purpose. In Chapter VII we showed how the agent's standpoint entailed Libertarian Indeterminism. If we now can show that Libertarian Indeterminism entails the agent's outlook on the immediate future, we will have demonstrated not merely the consistency of Libertarian Indeterminism with the responsibility created by choice, but its identity as well. It is usual for Libertarians to claim that indeterminacy is an indispensable condition of choice, but more unusual to contend explicitly as I do that it is a sufficient condition as well.

If the relationship between A, B^1 and the disjunction C^1 *or* C^2 provides a parallel for the relationship between past, present, and future from the agent's point of view, which of these terms is the event which the agent must predict in order to express his intention? Obviously it is B^1, the origin of this subsystem — because B^1 is the last member of the set of determinate existents in the subsystem before it joins the set of disjunctions. Accordingly, all the set of determinate terms originated by B^1 (i.e. in this instance A alone) must, with the exception of B^1 itself, be interpreted as belonging to the past, and B^1 must be included in the future along with the disjunctions or determinables which it originates.

But we have assumed here that the relationship between A, B^1, and the disjunction C^1 *or* C^2 is compatible with the agent's standpoint towards the future, whereas this is what has now to be proved. It is obvious to begin with that no term in its capacity as origin of a subsystem can be identified with the present. As we saw, the present is not an event but a date when some events are in the past and others in the future. If the present pertains to any event at all it can only do so, albeit indirectly, to the sum of events in the two different sets originating from the origin: i.e. the present consists of the pastness of one particular set of events and the futurity of yet another. One might, of course, be tempted to identify the origin with the so-called 'specious present': but that is a psychological or epistemological category, and not an ontological one. We are here concerned with what the origin is, and not with how it is known. One can without any logical absurdity identify, as I would, the specious present with the latest part of the past.

The only feasible question is whether the origin is the immediate past and not the immediate future. At first sight it might seem more natural to group the origin with the rest of the determinate existents which it originates, and exclude it from the group of less determinate existents (disjunctions) or determinate possibilities (disjuncts). In that case the origin would belong to the past, for the past is determinate. But on closer scrutiny there are better reasons for the reverse procedure. Each origin implies but is not implied by the set of determinate existents which it originates, e.g. B^1 implies but is not implied by A and C^1 implies but is not implied by B^1 and A. On the other hand, each origin both implies and is implied by the set of disjunctions which it originates, e.g. B^1 with respect to the disjunction C^1 *or* C^2, or C^1 with respect to the disjunction D^1 *or* D^2. Now, this is just the relation which from the agent's point of view holds between his most immediate and his less immediate future. What I am about to do entails the possibilities of action that lie before me in the future and likewise the possibility of these actions entails that I am about to do now what I am about to do. At the same time from the agent's point of view what I am about to do entails my past in so far as the circumstances of action (cf. Chapter VIII) are indispensable to my action. Furthermore, from the same standpoint, what I am about to do is not entailed by my past. Accordingly, we must interpret the set of equivalent terms including the origin as the future, and the set of determinate terms apart from the origin as the past. The origin, though determinate, is the immediate future and not the immediate past.

Libertarian Indeterminism, then, is a sufficient condition of responsibility for voluntary action, and not merely an indispensable one. It entails the kind of futurity which from the agent's point of view is peculiar to himself. From the agent's point of view his future is not merely incompletely conditioned by the past, but the fact of its being only incompletely conditioned by other events is what gives it its futurity. At first sight then an important question may still seem to be left unexplained. How is it that I am about to do one thing rather than the other things which I could equally well do? Or, alternatively, if B^1 implies and is implied by the disjunction C^1 *or* C^2, why should I say that C^1 rather than C^2 (or vice versa) is the future? If the futurity of events consists of their indeterminacy this question could have no answer, or so it might seem. It can, however, be answered up to a point. The fact that I am about to adopt one of the particular courses open to me rather than the others is certainly not determined by my past. It is determined by my remoter future — by the fact that the course I shall adopt determines and is determined by a further range of possibilities. B^1 for instance is not determined by A because A determines the disjunction B^1 *or* B^2. It is on the contrary determined by the disjunction C^1 *or* C^2. My going to catch the 9.30 a.m. rather than my doing something else is determined by the possibilities of action open to me when I reach my destination. The determinate character of the immediate future is determined by the particular range of possibilities of the more remote future and that in turn is determined by the still remoter future. If there were no remoter future consisting of a certain set of possibilities and excluding others, then I could have no determinate future. In fact the entire distinction between past and future would lapse.

Certain further implications of my argument remain to be examined. It may seem that to each agent there must correspond an indeterministic system of relations similar to the one I have constructed. Therefore I may seem faced with the unpleasant dilemma of maintaining, either that there is only one agent in the universe since there is only one process of time, or that there are several processes of time since there are more agents than one. Even if one interprets Einstein's theory of relativity as entailing that there are many different systems of time, we have not escaped the dilemma, since many of our acquaintances seem to belong to the same time system as ourselves.

Another difficulty is that other things besides my voluntary actions occur in the future. I can predict that I am going to sneeze involuntarily, or that there will be an eclipse of the sun at a certain date in the remote future.

Both these difficulties, however, are the result of forgetting that from his standpoint the agent's position in the universe is unique. It is not strictly parallel to the position of other agents. His future actions are not just one series out of a number of concurrent series of future events. If voluntary, they are done in consideration of the situation or the possibilities for the future which the situation permits. In deciding to catch the 9.30 a.m. the agent decides and acts in consideration of what he takes to be the facts about the future behaviour of trains, taxis, booking clerks, etc. etc. The future of everything else, objects and other agents, is, in other words, constitutive of the future of the agent from his private standpoint: nothing else is externally related to him. It is through this internal relation to him, accordingly, that events other than his actions have, from the standpoint of the agent, a temporal position in the past or future. Even where predictions are made on sufficient inductive grounds with no apparent reference to the agent, the grounds are insufficient for determining whether the inferred event takes place in the past or future, or even in some cases whether it takes place before or after the data. To determine the temporal reference of the grounds reference must be made to the agent. All this has been shown in greater detail in Chapters VII and VIII.

One important qualification to the preceding account remains to be made. As applied to the interpretation of human agency in the form it actually takes, this analysis presents a misleadingly simplified picture. It may suggest that the possibilities which constitute both the near and the remote future of any agent lie open before him in an obvious way. It may seem to suggest that even if at any moment he does not know what he will do in the remoter future, he at least can know what will be possible for him to do. Apart, however, from situations which are entirely familiar to us, we are in actual fact always acquiring new knowledge about ourselves and the world in which we live. Consequently, we have a continually changing idea of what respectively our past or future possibilities actually were or will be. Furthermore, this change in our conception of our possibilities is itself a contributing condition of their being possibilities. These facts do not, however, affect the basic validity of the principle in terms of which we have interpreted human agency.

There is, then, nothing left to explain if one can establish that

L

the future is incompletely determined by the past. It is precisely when one of two things is partially determined by the other in the way described above that it becomes possible to say of both that they are events and that the former will occur later than the other if the latter will occur. Such explanation as the occurrence of this rather than that partially determined event requires is entirely supplied by the possibilities and impossibilities for the remoter future to which it leads. The unresolved but specific possibilities of the remoter future both explain and are explained by the determinate form which the immediate future will take. There is nothing paradoxical about this conclusion, since it does justice to the essential lack of complete inductive warrant already indicated in Chapters VI and VII as peculiar to predictions in which the agent expresses purpose. We must never forget that for the agent the future includes what he is about to do as well as the future of his environment and that, further, the potentialities of his environment are constitutive of what he is about to do (Chapter VIII).

CHAPTER X

CONCLUSION

THE purpose throughout the preceding chapters has been to present a coherent form of Libertarian doctrine. So far I have dwelt mainly on questions of internal consistency. In concluding, however, I wish to consider, first the general adequacy of my account as an account of all the relevant facts, second the general significance for philosophy of the topic, and third the general nature and appropriateness of the methods I have employed. For convenience I start from the assumption that I have done what I set out to do. I have resolved the alleged paradox in Libertarian Indeterminism by an analysis of various concepts associated with the words 'responsibility', 'chance', 'accident', etc. The paradox depends upon the failure to see that in its formulation similar words have been used to express two different concepts which I have labelled 'explanatory responsibility' and 'narrative responsibility'. Further, I have shown that responsibility of the narrative kind for doing one thing rather than another must and can only exist where a full (as distinct from a limited) responsibility of the explanatory kind for doing one thing rather than another is absent.

I

Apart from questions of internal consistency, facts may seem to present Libertarians with difficulties in at least two important ways. These two I shall now consider.

(a) First: Libertarianism may seem to rule out the possibility of making definite and reliable predictions. Now we do predict with considerable accuracy and success. Indeed, the intelligent and voluntary behaviour of human beings is predictable as well as the behaviour of inanimate things. It won't do, of course, just to distinguish between the behaviour of purely physical objects, on the one hand, and the voluntary behaviour of persons, on the other, in order to confer indeterminacy upon the latter but withhold it from the former. Human agents, whatever else they are,

are physical objects, and their behaviour is causally connected with the behaviour of physical objects. Any indeterminacy in their behaviour must accordingly be communicated to the behaviour of the physical objects.

However, we must not forget that the indeterminacy required by Libertarianism is definitely a restricted indeterminacy. It cannot entail the complete unpredictability of physical events. The accuracy with which we can predict an eclipse of the sun, for instance, is not incompatible with indeterminacy in human behaviour. Even if we grant that every component of our solar system, or even the universe, is causally related to the behaviour of each human agent, none of our actions are, at the present stage of technology, likely to affect the behaviour of the sun to an extent that would make our prediction inaccurate. Of course, the possibility of turning the earth into an incandescent mass by means of nuclear fission or fusion is by this time imaginable. In this way the earth's relation to the sun might be altered and our former predictions about solar eclipses invalidated by human agency. However, the extent of human impotence in altering the course of nature remains considerable and widely recognized.

It might be objected that one can predict the behaviour of the ultimate constituents of matter with an extremely high degree of accuracy. Accordingly, since human beings are physical objects, it must in principle be possible to predict their behaviour with a similar degree of accuracy, even though as a matter of fact it may be impossible to compile the necessary data about ultimate particles. The high degree of accuracy possessed by such predictions could not possibly permit any indeterminacy in the occurrence of the actions between which the agent chooses. The range of inaccuracy would be imperceptible to human sense-organs unaided by scientific instruments, and normally we don't require scientific instruments to inform ourselves of the range of actions between which we must choose.

One might reply that it is just in the realm of sub-atomic particles that the principle of indeterminacy has its most striking applications. It is impossible, for instance, to determine the momentum and the position of electrons with equal degrees of accuracy. Accuracy in the measurement of any one of these variables involves a comparative inaccuracy in the measurement of the other. It is, accordingly, perfectly consistent with the find-ings of science to hold that there is a restricted indeterminacy in the universe.[1] But in different ways this restriction may seem both too great and too small. Too great, because if there is restricted indeterminacy in the behaviour of the ultimate constituents of all physical matter, then everything in the physical universe is an agent, according to the thesis of the previous chapters. Too small, because the indeterminacy which the Libertarian wishes to attri-bute to the human agent is much less restricted. Depending upon whether one decides to catch a plane one may on a given day find oneself in places as physically separate as, say, Edinburgh or Singapore. How can the equal possibility of two such widely different courses be explained in terms of the minute indeter-minacies exhibited by electrons and their aggregates? Neither difficulty to my mind is insuperable.

To make a hard and fast distinction between things which are merely physical and things which are people who act voluntarily may seem difficult if we try and reconcile indeterminacy in the sub-atomic world with the thesis of the previous chapters. If restricted indeterminacy is a sufficient condition of agency, and also is exhibited by the ultimate constituents of physical matter, then everything must be capable of voluntary action. But even so, I see no reason why we should insist on such a hard and fast distinction. May there not be degrees of agency depending upon degrees of indeterminacy? After all we do recognize such grada-tions when we compare the actions of human agents with the actions of lower forms of life. Furthermore, we experience diffi-culty in distinguishing animal from vegetable, and even animate from inanimate. Human beings may owe their principal difference from other things just to the comparative wideness of the range of actions open to them. We might suppose that the function of the human nervous system is to superimpose, one upon the other, the indeterminacies in behaviour of some of the constituents of our bodies — to trigger off larger indeterminacies by means of the smaller ones. This is, presumably, a hypothesis capable, when more fully elaborated, of empirical confirmation.

[1] For the logical inevitability of some indeterminacy of prediction in any system of mechanics, classical or quantum, cf. K. Popper, 'Indeterminism in Quantum Physics', *The British Journal for the Philosophy of Science*, vol. I, nos. 2 and 3, 1950.

I am not at all sure, however, that the indeterminacies exhibited by electrons really require that I should speculate about whether electrons, or the objects they constitute, must be agents of essentially the same kind as human beings. The indeterminacy in the observed behaviour of sub-atomic particles seems, in many cases at least, to be due to the fact that the observer must act upon them in order to observe them. His measuring instruments alter the behaviour of the thing measured. Consequently, this kind of indeterminacy is consistent with quite a different sort of hypothesis about the human nervous system. The behaviour of the constituents of matter, on this hypothesis, is not normally indeterministic. But in the human nervous system, and perhaps in others, special conditions exist which produce indeterminacy of behaviour. This indeterminacy may affect the *observed* behaviour of the material particles which exhibit the 'complementarity' phenomena described by Bohr,[1] although their actual behaviour is not indeterministic. It is not, however, my intention here to arbitrate between the available hypotheses, nor even to formulate them exhaustively.

Before leaving the question of consistency between Libertarianism and physical science I would like, however, to consider very briefly the possible relevance of entropy. The universe as it ages shows an increasing randomness, disorganization of energy, or entropy. Accordingly, the stage of entropy serves as a criterion for determining the temporal position relative to each other of two different phases of the same physical set-up. Entropy is a sort of temporal signpost. Now, I have no clear understanding of the concept of energy as used by physicists and consequently no clear understanding of the concept of disorganized energy. If, however, by 'an increase of randomness' they mean 'an increase in the number of dispositions of the universe that are possible at any one moment and a decrease in the probability of any one of these possibilities' the relevance of entropy to my argument must be fully apparent.[2] In the previous chapter I have maintained that this increase in the number of possibilities is not merely a criterion for determining serial order in time but the relation from which

---

[1] *Albert Einstein: Philosopher-Scientist*, p. 223 (Library of Living Philosophers, ed. Schilp).

[2] Cf. Eddington, *The Nature of the Physical World*, chap. IV.

the temporal series is derivative. Consequently, subject to the qualifications I have made, the presence of entropy provides empirical confirmation for my argument.[1] It does not establish it, of course, because a logical analysis cannot be established by empirical means.

This only completes one phase, however, in our reply to the question whether Libertarianism is consistent with prediction. Objections are often based not upon the predictability of physical occurrences in general but of human behaviour in particular. We make quite a habit of predicting the behaviour of social groups and the voluntary actions of individuals.

Predictions about social groups, indeed, are often based upon our knowledge of the social organization of a society, and those about individuals upon our knowledge of their character. These predictions, however, are seldom specific to the last degree. I don't predict exactly how many students will come to my lecture tomorrow, nor who they will be, but only that the majority will turn up, because there are no holidays, nor epidemics, etc., and because I know several things about them, such as their anxiety to pass examinations or their willingness to be bored. Provided the indeterminacy of behaviour in a number of individuals is restricted, it will always be possible to make reliable predictions about the groups they comprise. In much the same way we make

---

[1] In his *Philosophie der Raum-Zeit-Lehre* (recently translated as *The Philosophy of Space and Time*) and in his posthumously published *The Direction of Time* Hans Reichenbach has interpreted entropy in terms of the frequency instead of the disjunctive account of probability. By means of this interpretation he has given an alternative analysis of the serial order of time. It is, however, much less economical than the analysis I give above. In order to derive serial temporal order from probability relations his frequency interpretation of probability compels him to distinguish the order of between-ness among events as more basic than their serial temporal order, and to derive the order of between-ness from the one-one connections between events postulated by the laws of classical mechanics. Secondly, he has to account quite separately for the distinction between past, present, and future, as expressed by the temporal inflections of verbs (cf. above Chapter IX). The disjunctive analysis, on the other hand, accounts for temporal between-ness, serial order, and the temporal inflections of verbs all in one.

Apart from being uneconomical his analysis is *prima facie* circular.

(*a*) If the non-statistical laws of classical mechanics are less basic than statistical laws how can the order of temporal between-ness which depends upon the former be fundamental to the frequency interpretation of statistical laws?

(*b*) The only sense in which an event B can be regarded as temporally between A and C requires the fulfilment of three conditions. (i) B is simultaneous neither with A nor C; (ii) if it is before C then it is after A; and (iii) if it is after C then it is before A.

Accordingly even though it may be left indeterminate whether B is before or after C, the serial temporal relations of *before* and *after* are basic to the relation of temporal between-ness and not derivable from it.

reliable predictions about gases when we regard them as collec-
tions of individual molecules. We do not know how each individual molecule will behave but we know they will observe the
limits which are formulated in the laws of mechanics. Such knowledge is sufficient for the purpose of predicting with a high degree
of probability the behaviour of the collection of molecules as a
whole. The analogy between gases and social groups is not, of
course, complete even in relevant respects. Other factors which
determine the latter will come into evidence when we turn to
predictions about individual persons.

Many of our predictions about an individual's behaviour are
simply based upon our knowledge of his intentions. This may be
derived either from observation of his actions or simply from his
statements of intention. Now no Libertarian would wish to deny
that an agent's intentions condition his actions in some way, nor
is there any reason why he should deny it. Of course, if he does
treat intentions as causal conditions of actions, the Libertarian
must suppose that indeterminacy in agency is antecedent to the
intention. But there are alternative accounts of this sort of condition as in Chapter VII.

Often, however, it must be admitted, we predict individual
behaviour sometime before any specific intention has been formed
by the agent. We rely upon our knowledge of his character. The
concept of character, however, is somewhat amorphous. In some
of its applications it seems very similar to that of psychological
habit. If we respond to a certain kind of situation in a certain kind
of way sufficiently often we will create a psychological tendency
to continue responding in that way in similar situations. The
Libertarian, however, has no need to deny the existence
of such tendencies. The limits of indeterminacy which he
postulates might be psychological as well as physical. In
any case, even supposing some of our actions are entirely
the product of habit, there are many of our actions which are
not habitual.

On the other hand character often is supposed to consist of a
more reflective, less mechanical, pattern in a man's behaviour
than habit. There may be a peculiar kind of set in his deliberate
purposes in accordance with which he invariably behaves in a
certain manner. But is this set itself deliberative or purposive? I

think in many discussions it has been wrongly assimilated to the habitual or more mechanical form of behaviour. One must admit, however, that the set in an individual's choices, which we call his character, is seldom as deliberate as the actions he performs in accordance with the set. Pre-eminently it is the specific properties of the action which are fully deliberate, and not the general characteristics which predispose the agent in that particular action's favour. It is, however, a familiar fact that we often apprehend only dimly the more general characteristics of a phenomenon. Someone with a good but relatively untutored ear can recognize a certain composition as Mozart's at first hearing without being able to define his criterion for recognition. Similarly, an agent may choose in doing a particular action to realize some general characteristic without being able properly to distinguish the general from the particular aspect.

In so choosing he may even feel the sort of compulsion which moved Luther to say 'Ich kann nicht anders'. An overwhelming revulsion towards any other course may seem to well up from the very ground of his being. This way of putting it, however, is metaphorical and a trifle narcissistic. As a simple fact it is part of the discovery of one's own personality to bring to reflective consciousness the general course one has espoused and of which one has hitherto had only a particularized awareness in one's particular responses to particular situations. One's character, then, or the set in one's purposes, is not a predetermined cast in which one's actions are moulded. The character of his actions has been chosen by the agent in choosing to do various characteristic actions, even though he is unaware that he has performed these actions for the sake of their common characteristic. Consequently, a Libertarian can recognize that we base predictions about action upon knowledge of character as cheerfully as he can recognize that we can predict an action upon knowing that the agent has chosen or intended to do it.

However, one must not ignore the influence of genetic factors in the formation of character. There is evidence that where one member of a pair of identical twins has had a criminal record, the other twin has had, in a very high proportion of the cases investigated, a remarkably similar criminal record. Where the twins, on the other hand, are not identical, there is no noteworthy correla-

tion.[1] The significance of such cases, however, may well be superficial. Probably criminals are more subject to various kinds
of compulsions or psycho-somatic defects which limit their freedom than any other class of person. Consequently the fact that
criminal identical twins have almost identical records does not
sufficiently indicate that the behaviour of non-criminal identical
twins is almost identical. An independent investigation of the
non-criminal class is really required. In any case the Libertarian
can admit that the limitations to indeterminacy are inherent in the
agent as well as in the circumstances in which the agent acts.
Accordingly, he can willingly admit that temperament, for instance, is largely dependent upon genetic factors and that consequently the actions to which an agent's temperament gives rise
are genetically determined in part. But there is no reason why he
should concede more than this.

(b) The second apparent difficulty for Libertarianism consists
in the phenomena of second-sight or precognition. These may
seem to suggest that the future is every bit as determinate as the
past. Not so much has been made of this difficulty in recent discussions of the problem of free will, perhaps because the scientific
respectability of precognition is believed still to be in the balance.
The difficulty has, however, theological precedents in the doctrine
of predestination according to which God has foreknowledge of
everything including our ultimate destiny and given sufficient
godliness we can share his convictions on the last matter as well.
Many may feel content to wait until the weight of evidence for
precognition becomes irresistible before considering its implications with any seriousness. But this attitude is a little bit crass for
three reasons. First, the resistance to the evidence for precognition
stems at least partly from the apparent difficulty of accommo-
dating it in our normal conceptual framework. Therefore, questions of conceptual consistency should be entered into without
delay and with all the diligence we can muster. Secondly, whether
we remain aloof or not, the fact remains that many people, possibly
all, though some more frequently than others, do have apparently
precognitive experiences. If one is gifted or afflicted in this way

---

[1] See C. E. M. Joad, *Guide to the Philosophy of Morals and Politics*, p. 235, also cited by
M. Cranston, *Freedom*, p. 161.

one remains worried, and sometimes disorientated if they are sufficiently disturbing, even while aware of the various hypotheses which explain them away. One may find oneself, for instance, taking ineffective measures to avoid the apparently precognized event. Thirdly, none of the explanations alternative to that of precognition succeed in allaying the most significant impression made by many of these experiences. What impresses is not so much the identity in cognitive detail between the event as supposedly precognized and its actual occurrence. When the the 'precognition' takes place during sleep, as so often it does, this identity can be remarkably inexact. Many experiences, taken as experiences which involve one personally, have a peculiar quite unique feel about them which is almost inexpressible in words. It is principally this identity in feel which arouses recognition when the 'precognized' event actually occurs. It can, of course, be explained away by supposing that one has really had the feel of the event for the first time and only imagines that one recognizes it. But when this has been said one continues to imagine, and one may feel uneasy about the claims of Libertarianism. The fact that it is difficult if not impossible to devise public checks on this supposed recognition does not justify our discounting it.

Let us then take precognitive experience at its face value and examine more fully the relevant implications to find in particular whether these are really inconsistent with Libertarianism. One fact of importance is that so far as the evidence goes we do not precognize the whole of our future. Why is this? It may have the same sort of explanation as the fact that we do not remember the whole of our past. The reason for this seems to be psychological or physiological rather than any incompleteness in our past. We may remember, forget, and remember again the same event several times over. This suggests that there are events actually in the past even at the point where there is a gap in one's memory. On the other hand, we precognize very much less of the future than we remember of the past. Of course, we might conceivably precognize, 'forget', and precognize again the same event in the future. But the important point is that if we do this at all, we do it very much less than we do the comparable things to the past. It must be admitted that probably we have many more precognitions than we recognize. Many may take place in dreams which we later forget. But it remains plausible that the apparent infrequency of our precognitions is real and at least partly due to an incompleteness in the future rather than to a gap in our awareness. Much of the future may not be determinate enough to be precognized. May Libertarians not congratulate themselves on this residue of indeterminacy?

This issue may seem to depend upon whether the future can indeed be partially determinate and partially indeterminate. We might argue that it must be either one or the other, but not partially both. The fact that we can precognize anything at all shows, it might be argued, that the distinction between past, present, and future is not fundamental to the order of events. It must show that all things which ever have occurred, are occurring, or will occur do exist (in a timeless sense of 'exist'). They are (timeless copula) in temporal relations of antecedence, simultaneity, or subsequence to each other. The apparent emptiness which we describe as 'future' is a mere epistemological emptiness. In any act of knowing we happen, for the most part to be ignorant of a certain batch of events that exist (timelessly) after the act, and we label this batch 'the future' to distinguish it from other batches of which we are not ignorant. But our ignorance, or partial ignorance, of this batch is a purely contingent limitation of human nature carrying no logical necessity whatever.

Actually, however, we need not decide whether the future can be partially determinate and partially indeterminate because we can account for the fact that precognitive phenomena are intermittent even on the supposition that the future is entirely indeterminate. Nor in order to do this need we attribute them to coincidence or to later imagination. A precognized event can simply be interpreted as an event which may or may not occur but as having, irrespective of whether it occurs, an indeterminate temporal position or lack of order in the series of possible or actual occurrences.

In the preceding chapter I have argued that the distinction between past, present, and future is as basic to temporal order as that between before and after, for they both are derived from the same relation. The compactness of the diagram I used for this purpose now achieves its proper significance in the explanation of precognition.

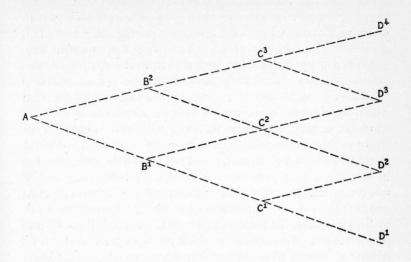

If the temporal order of a set of events depends upon a certain relationship it follows that where this relationship is defective in asymmetry or transitivity, or connexity, temporal order will be replaced by temporal disorder. All three of these properties, we saw, must characterize any relation which orders perfectly. Now one of the ways in which time may be disorderly is represented by the compactness of our diagram. This has produced a failure in the asymmetry of the relation between certain of the terms. B^2 is the referent of a one-many relation with C^2 and C^3, but likewise C^2 is the referent of a one-many relation with B^1 and B^2. Perhaps the symmetry is brought out more clearly if we say that not only is B^2 the indispensable and sufficient condition of a disjunction between C^2 and something else, but that C^2 is likewise an indispensable and sufficient condition of a disjunction between B^2 and something else. If we express the symmetry in this way we should notice, however, that this sort of symmetry in the relation between B^2 and C^2 is reinforced, by a similar sort of symmetry between B^1 and C^2. Not only is B^1 the indispensable and sufficient condition of a disjunction between C^2 and something else, but also C^2 is an indispensable and sufficient condition of a disjunction between B^1 and something else. We can see, of course, that the bare distinction between symmetry and asymmetry isn't really sufficiently sensitive to all the possible ways in which relations apart from the one-one type may differ from their converses, but there is no need to enter into these niceties here.

Now if temporal order is derivable from the relation of one-many necessary connection, there might be certain temporal anomalies brought about by a defective asymmetry of the kind which the diagram represents. If we interpret C^2 as an event, it would in certain respects be successor to A and to either B^1 or B^2. In so far as it is a relatum of a one-many relationship of which either B^1 or B^2 is the referent, it succeeds A and the latter two. But in so far as it is the referent of a one-many relation to B^1 and B^2 it is temporally prior to either of these, and, furthermore, it must compete with A for the position of immediate antecedence to B^1 or B^2. Of course, the respects in which C^2 succeeds B^1 or B^2 preponderate over the respects in which it comes prior to them. C^2 relative to B^1 and B^2 is disjunctively related to C^1 and C^3 respectively. Accordingly the respects in which it succeeds either B^1 or B^2 are twice as strong as the respects in which it precedes them.

The application of the diagram to the explanation of precognition should now be apparent. It explains why the same event, e.g. one represented by C^2, may seem later in time than another event, e.g. B^1 or B^2, and yet to compete for the same position of antecedence before B^1 or B^2 as is occupied by A. In so far then as this sort of situation is the sort of situation we describe as 'precognitive', the analysis of precognition given here is adequate. It also accounts for the relative patchiness of precognition since in our diagram D^2 and D^3 are the only other terms in a similar position to C^2. Other diagrams are possible, of course, in which the occurrence of such anomalies are less or more frequent.

There are, however, an indefinite number of aspects of precognitive experience which in this explanation have been or may seem to have been left out of account. No doubt the explanation of some of these would require auxiliary hypotheses. The whole matter invites a more careful weighing than I can conveniently here perform. My provisional estimate, is that I have attended to the kernel of precognitive experience.

The diagram has one further implication for precognitive experience which I can now make explicit. On this interpretation the event precognized will not necessarily occur. In the diagram the possibility of C^1 and C^3 relative to A is not removed. A does not necessitate C^2 as against C^1 and C^3, although on the other hand C^2 does necessitate A. If, then, a necessary condition of genuine precognitive experience is that the event cognized must necessarily occur then the diagram fails to account for precognitive experience. Now it may seem that the actual occurrence of an event is our principal reason for saying that an event is 'precognized'. But the strict conclusion is merely that the use of a veridical term like 'precognized' may be question-begging. It may be that all one needs to explain is why an experience which we have actually had seems in a manner to have occupied a previous position in time. There may be no need to infer from the fact that it has occupied in this manner a previous position in time that its subsequent occurrence is necessary. All we may need to suppose is that, whether it occurs or not, it has in certain limited respects an indeterminate temporal position; for, of course, events which may possibly occur have a relative temporal order as well as events that do occur. On this interpretation, then, precognition is not the direct experience at an earlier moment of an event that is definitely located at a later moment. It is, on the contrary, an indefinitely located experience of an event: and this experience need not be one which actually has taken place or will actually take place — it may be one that could have taken place or could be about to take place.

On my interpretation there is, nevertheless, something approximating towards necessity about a 'precognized' event. From the diagram one can see at a glance that C^2, for instance, is more probable relative to A than either C^1 or C^3. In fact it is twice as probable as either C^1 or C^3 taken individually. Accordingly, I can maintain that 'precognitive' experience gives some indication of what *will* happen as against what *may* happen later. In a modified way, then, the use of the adjective 'precognitive' has a justification, though a 'precognitive' experience is no *certain* guarantee for the later occurrence of an event.

I shall refrain, here, from investigating alternative diagrams which by representing a slightly different nexus of relation would appear to endow precognitive experience with greater predictive power. It is sufficient for my present purpose to have shown that the possibility of precognition *follows from* a specialized form of Libertarianism. It is not merely *consistent with* the latter. If we investigated further, I think several freak, or more esoteric, temporal experiences of other kinds would be found likewise explicable by means of other specialized forms. But since the general principle of explanation should by this time be obvious I shan't postpone the conclusion of my central thesis for the sake of a digression.

2

Has the topic of this analysis any very great significance for ethics or other branches of philosophy? Recent writers on ethics such as Stevenson[1] and Hare[2] have tended to treat their views on free will, if they have any, as somewhat of a luxury. The issue, they seem to feel, has little urgency and in no way imperils their more important views on the logic of 'right', 'ought', and 'good'. Where other branches of philosophy apart from ethics are concerned the issue may well seem to have outlived its significance. It was a live issue when doctrines of predestination or theological determinism engaged the general interest. They no longer do so. It was a live issue in the heyday of classical physics. But now physicists make fewer assumptions. It was a live issue when Freud was a scandal. But now he seems no more than a pioneer in a science, the basic concepts of which we must continue to scrutinize and revise. Why should the subject of free will excite us? Hasn't it gone a bit musty?

We must not, however, let the longevity of the subject obscure its importance. It has indeed been extremely unfortunate in its history. Too often it has featured as the sticking point beyond which the more scrupulous have felt reluctant to screw the various extrapolatory fads of their day. In consequence they have tended to affirm free will in terms of the very concepts by which it seemed most imperilled. The *deus ex machina* is invoked to rescue us from his machine. Too seldom has any effort been made to analyse the concepts specific and peculiar to agency. Philosophers with insistent intellects such as Kant, and Bradley in his *Collected Essays*, have indeed allowed some light to percolate into the subject by straining the mechanistic categories by which they were

---

[1] *Ethics and Language*, pp. 312ff.   [2] *The Language of Morals*, p. vi.

bedevilled almost to the point of transparency. In consequence they are slighted as muddled or obscure. Within recent years, however, a fresh approach has become evident in, for instance, the realization that expressions of intention are in some way peculiar.

The importance of the subject is undeniable if only because it concerns the understanding of ourselves and the sort of world in which we are accommodated. This perhaps could be shown better if we were to enter into the ethical implications of the issue. I have so far, however, shown a marked lack of concern with ethics. This may seem the more remarkable since many Libertarians have looked upon themselves as the guardians and preservers of that department. Morality, they suppose, depends for its applicability upon the freedom of the will in the indeterministic interpretation of freedom. I am not disposed to deny this. I merely think there is very little point in affirming it at the present juncture of philosophical thought. At the moment the precise status of predicates like 'right', 'ought', and 'good' is controversial and their metaphysical implications in consequence correspondingly unsettled.

My silence on this subject, then, has been due to the conviction that we shall not discover very much more about the logic of 'right', 'ought', and 'good' until we discover more about the logic of statements about actions or agents in general. The maxim 'Ought implies can' supplies a conceptual bridge between ethics and metaphysics which moralists should cross from the metaphysical side.

We need only reflect how prevalent in past ethical writings are distinctions between actions and intentions and motives, or between actions and their consequences. Almost invariably they are misconceived as some of my conclusions in preceding chapters are enough to show. Or consider again the parallel between the mechanistic model of action as proceeding from a composition of independent desires which compel and the intuitionist's realm of independent intrinsic values which attract. Then there are the contemporary moralists who are still so tickled with their hunch that the use of language for describing is different from its use in evaluating, advising, commending, recommending, appraising, prescribing, and so on and so forth, that they have forgotten to

M

give adequate attention to what the significant differences, if any, between all these activities happen to be. What is it, for instance, that distinguishes a world in which the former activity alone is applicable, if that makes sense, from a world in which the latter are applicable as well? Until questions like this are satisfactorily solved, the hunch is no more than a hunch depending for its ascendancy merely upon the fact that it hadn't occurred unequivocally to our predecessors. The gate across the conceptual bridge 'Ought implies can' has indeed been unlocked. We need no longer feel quite so puzzled by Kant's question 'How can reason be practical?' But the traffic hasn't properly begun.

Nor must we forget that our ethical differences are more than a matter of interpreting a homogeneous and universally acceptable morality. They reflect to a considerable extent differences between moralities. Praise and blame, for instance, function more as tools of instruction or compulsion for the authoritarian whereas for the liberal they become less gross. Their vehicles are viewed by the latter as primarily modes of personal intercourse and no longer carry quite the same weight of interference. There is a pervasive difference of emphasis here even where content remains substantially the same. Differences of this kind stem from conflicting conceptions of man and signify the metaphysical shallowness or profundity of the moralities they typify. Metaphysics and the issue of free will in particular must come first.

So much, then, for the ethical relevance of the subject. But in addition I hope I have succeeded in suggesting and in some cases in showing how it is more central to some of the major non-ethical preoccupations of philosophy than is commonly suspected. An understanding of freedom and responsibility provides an analysis of the concepts of substance, personal identity as a self-determining unity, and time. It may further offer a clue to the analysis of other equally important concepts which in the course of my argument I have had rather lamely to postulate but now shall not specify so as not to give hostages to the future.

3

I have, it may be observed, been treating my subject as primarily ontological in scope and only secondarily as psychological. I have treated choice as the sort of thing we *have* or by which we are *faced*, rather than as one of our mental processes distinguishable from the other volitional or conative processes in which we engage. As I have tried to indicate, this is a matter of emphasis rather than a limitation in subject. It can be explained by the importance I have placed upon the distinction between the agent's and the alien standpoint. When we take the agent's standpoint towards his future voluntary action in abstraction from the alien standpoint the nature of our inquiry becomes ontological. Choice is, then, the thing by which he is faced. When we include the alien standpoint which the agent in acting takes towards other agents, and himself regarded impersonally, the inquiry must become psychological as well. I must admit, however, that the psychological sections of my discussion are often sketchy and incidental to the main ontological drift. This is because the ontological aspect throws more light upon the psychological than vice versa, and because at the same time it is less familiar. In not making an adequate allowance for the distinction between the agent's and the alien standpoint most writers on the subject have given too great prominence to psychological categories at a stage in the inquiry where they are inappropriate.

Throughout these chapters I have in effect given the dualism between the agent's and the alien standpoint the ultimate status traditionally reserved for a dualism between mind and matter. Standpoint, of course, seems to be a mental category; but I have in fact reduced the difference between the agent from his own and from the alien standpoint respectively to the difference between an indeterminacy which may be constituted by indeterminacies or determinacies among the standing conditions and an indeterminacy which so constitutes an indeterminacy. This reduction, of course, demands systematic application beyond the immediate vicinity of intention, choice, and deliberation to the more theoretical mental concepts which these practical concepts seem indeed to involve. To undertake such a task simultaneously with my analysis of responsibility might, however, distract the attention on which each of these rather difficult topics makes rather exclusive demands.

My analysis has raised and left unsettled questions less fundamental to psychology than this. In a fuller treatment I would have to be more explicit about the role of consciousness in action. More, for instance, needs to be said about the extent to which conscious processes are themselves actions and the extent to which they are merely activities involved in action. More has also to be said about the peculiarly emotive, even visceral, character of our desires and aversions, or again about the distinction between acting deliberately, spontaneously, impulsively, and by habit. I could pass on to these questions by way of tying up loose ends left by preceding chapters, but in the absence of some decision on the more fundamental question the effect would be unsatisfying.

So much for scope and its perspective. I conclude on the stultifying topic of method. It is inevitable that I should have paid some attention to the way in which certain expressions are used, but I would hesitate on the strength of this to describe my method of analysis as 'linguistic': 'logical' or 'conceptual' might be more appropriate, even if a trifle redundant in this context. In any case my inquiry has not been confined to the area of *ordinary* linguistic usage. At no time did I wish to suggest that the philosophical problem has arisen from the misuse of ordinary language. Some philosophical problems arise simply in the attempt to enrich language with a precision which for certain purposes it ordinarily lacks.

A language may be called upon to express subtleties which it did not orignally envisage; or it may have to assimilate special vocabularies disseminated by new learning. One could perhaps avoid making any explicit innovations in language in the form of vocabulary or rules of use if one had correspondingly precise *implicit* knowlege of the ordinary context to which a specific vocabulary and grammar was adequate. Provided, then, one cares more for the primitive purity of our language than its usefulness one will choose to remain dumb whenever the context becomes more complex. Thus there are perfectly ordinary uses of the words 'cause' and 'responsible' which need not even suggest the paradox of Libertarianism.

Ordinarily it may be the case that when a man says 'John is responsible for that' he uses 'responsible' more for what Hart calls ascriptive purposes than for the narrative purposes to which I have confined it. Ordinarily when a man uses the word 'cause' he is as likely to use it of an object as of an event and still more likely to use it of that part of the total conditions which is most directly controllable from his point of view. It is only when we begin to use the word 'responsible' for the precondition of ascriptive responsibility and the word 'cause' for the sort of relationship between events that occur in accordance with scientific laws, that the problem arises whether or not to identify responsibility with causation and whether or not responsibility is consistent with indeterminate causal relationships. But the problem has to arise, for this is the only way in which we can become aware of the limitations to the context within which certain uses are legitimate.

Philosophical method is, indeed, rather undercharacterized if one describes it simply as analysis of some sort. Philosophical perplexity is not simply the misconstruction of some clearly delimitable conceptual nexus. If it was we could hope for the 'once and for all' sort of analysis which philosophers so often promise but seldom seem able to bring off. The hope is vain because concepts are open, not, or not only, in the sense that they lack precise unity, but in the sense that they are incomplete. A concept is always amenable to enrichment in the form of closer or more comprehensive integration with other concepts. In consequence there is always the possibility of relative progress and legitimate controversy, though there can be no final settlement: and each advance is subject to drastic revision.

INDEX

INDEX